Raising a Whole Child

by the same author

What Color is Monday?
How Autism Changed One Family for the Better
Carrie Cariello
ISBN 978 1 84905 727 1
eISBN 978 1 78450 094 8

of related interest

Nurturing Your Autistic Young Person
A Parent's Handbook to Supporting Newly Diagnosed Teens and Pre-Teens
Cathy Wassell
Foreword by Emily Burke
Illustrated by Eliza Fricker
ISBN 978 1 83997 111 2
eISBN 978 1 83997 112 9

The #ActuallyAutistic Guide to Building Independence
A Handbook for Teens, Young Adults, and Those Who Care About Them
Jennifer Brunton and Jenna Gensic
ISBN 978 1 80501 000 5
eISBN 978 1 80501 001 2

Raising a Whole Child

A family guide to supporting autistic children into adulthood

Carrie Cariello

Jessica Kingsley Publishers
London and Philadelphia

First published in Great Britain in 2025 by Jessica Kingsley Publishers
An imprint of John Murray Press

1

Copyright © Carrie Cariello 2025

The right of Carrie Cariello to be identified as the Author of the Work has been asserted by her in accordance with the Copyright, Designs and Patents Act 1988.

Front cover image source: Shutterstock®.

All rights reserved. No part of this publication may be reproduced, stored in a retrieval system, or transmitted, in any form or by any means without the prior written permission of the publisher, nor be otherwise circulated in any form of binding or cover other than that in which it is published and without a similar condition being imposed on the subsequent purchaser.

A CIP catalogue record for this title is available from the British Library and the Library of Congress

ISBN 978 1 80501 111 8
eISBN 978 1 80501 112 5

Printed and bound in the United States by Integrated Books International

Jessica Kingsley Publishers' policy is to use papers that are natural, renewable and recyclable products and made from wood grown in sustainable forests. The logging and manufacturing processes are expected to conform to the environmental regulations of the country of origin.

Jessica Kingsley Publishers
Carmelite House
50 Victoria Embankment
London EC4Y 0DZ

www.jkp.com

John Murray Press
Part of Hodder & Stoughton Ltd
An Hachette Company

The authorised representative in the EEA is Hachette Ireland, 8 Castlecourt Centre, Dublin 15, D15 XTP3, Ireland (email: info@hbgi.ie)

Contents

Introduction 7

1. Paper Cut Days: Autism and Grief 13
2. Autism and Food: How to Have Success at the Dinner Table. 23
3. How to Prepare for Family Gatherings. 35
4. Autism Siblings. 49
5. Strategies for Money and Budgeting. 57
6. Puberty 65
7. How to Give the Sex Talk. 93
8. Autism, Dating, and Social Media 103
9. Raising a Whole Child 115
10. Tips for Marriage 129
11. Finding a Program after High School 143
12. The Road to Independence (or at Least to Moving Out). 159

Discussion Questions 173

Introduction

The late afternoon sun dances across my desk. It's more orange than yellow. Here in New Hampshire, autumn is well on its way.

I lean back in my chair, a Word document open on my laptop. It's blank.

I feel first-day-of-school nervous. Going-into-labor nervous. Except instead of balancing on the ledge of newly sharpened pencils or sweet-smelling baby clothes I am trying to cobble a few words together that may turn into something bigger.

I am supposed to be writing a guidebook right now. It's what we all agreed upon—the publisher, the editor, me. A how-to manual about raising a child with autism. Advice for how get through puberty and keep your marriage intact and not lose your ever-loving marbles through it all.

I decided to write the Introduction first. This seems like a logical starting point, except I rarely begin my books this way. I like to jump around—let one chapter lead me to the next. I often arrange the table of contents last, just before I figure out the title.

To me, the introduction of a book is a little like an invitation to a party. It explains the theme. It lays out the cast of characters and gives you an idea of what to expect.

What can I tell you?

My name is Carrie. I was named after my mother's cousin. Her other cousin was named Alveena. In retrospect, Carrie suits me a little better.

My husband is Joe, formally Joseph. For reasons that have never been explained to me, he has no middle name. Perhaps it's an Italian thing. Or maybe by the time he rolled around—the last of six kids—they'd simply run out of ideas.

Joe and I have been married for twenty-five years.

We have five kids.

Our firstborn, Joseph, is twenty. He is a junior in college. He is gentle and sweet, but he will eat your leftovers without asking.

Our second son Jack is nineteen. He just started his second year in a residential space. He takes two classes at a nearby college.

Charlie is seventeen, all dark eyes and racing heart. I liken him to a puppy, or a kite. Open the door and out he flies.

INTRODUCTION

Our daughter Rose is sixteen. She just got her driver's license. Watching her back out of the driveway, hot tears pricked my eyelids, knowing I'll probably never need to pick her up from crew practice or a babysitting job again. I always enjoyed the time in the car with her, even if I was late a lot of the time.

Our youngest son Henry is fourteen. He is taller than me, but I still think of him as a little boy. He hates when I say this.

By the time you read this book, they will be a year older, perhaps more. That's how publishing works. It freezes your family in time.

Jack was diagnosed with autism when he was eighteen months old. It was a chilly day in November. He was wearing overalls.

I called Joe as soon as we got home. This was 2004, and cell phones were big, clunky devices that weighed down your purse. Talking from the car was impossible.

We lived in Buffalo, New York. I took the highway home from downtown. I got off on the exit and drove through our neighborhood. I felt drained, but also calm.

I pulled into our driveway and parked near the back door. Jack had fallen asleep in his car seat. I carried him inside and put him on the couch. I started a *Baby Einstein* DVD for him to watch. He loved those DVDs. I needed to think. Yet my mind was empty, like a cloudless sky.

Suddenly I felt nauseous and hot. Stripping off my coat, I walked through the dining room and into the kitchen.

I leaned against the small table in the breakfast nook and picked up the phone.

I dialed Joe's number. He paused after I delivered the news. Then he suggested we order pizza for dinner. And we did.

The truth is, we had no idea of the path we were about to travel. Looking back, perhaps that was for the best.

I don't know how to write a guidebook.

I can only tell you all the ways we tried to navigate every facet of life alongside autism—religion, adolescence, social media, online dating. Mealtimes, post-high school programs, medication, marriage.

I can only write about the way autism offered our family a newfound opportunity to reinvent ourselves. It brought us back to the basics: dinner around the table at night, dance parties in the playroom, adventures on Sunday afternoons.

I can only explain how we tried to stretch this boy Jack without breaking him. How, again and again, we stretched and nearly broke ourselves.

How we surrendered to a life we didn't ask for, but we love all the same.

INTRODUCTION

When it comes to autism, there is no instruction manual. There is no formula.

Nineteen years later, I rediscover this truth all the time.

There are only failed attempts, moments of mercy, offers of forgiveness, and the gritty determination to begin once more.

To me, good writing means you'll see a piece of yourself inside my words.

Great writing, however, will infinitesimally change the way you live your own story.

Though I have no assumptions about where I fall on this sliding scale of letters to page, I offer them to you anyway.

Take what you need. Leave the rest.

Perhaps you'll feel validated, curious, upset, confused, hopeful.

I hope you'll read about something we tried—timers at the dinner table, emotional thermometers taped on the wall, couples' counseling when we felt like we were becoming unmoored—and you'll try it yourself.

And maybe you or your kiddo or your marriage will inch just the smallest bit forward. Ten more minutes in a restaurant, a meltdown that was shorter than the last, stolen kisses in the hallway.

And you'll share this tiniest piece of yourself to another mother, sister, father, husband.

After all, one story begets another.

All we can do is learn from each other.

All we have is each other.

It's getting dark now, as the sun begins its descent into the dusky night. In a few minutes, I'll get up and head into the kitchen to make dinner. It was always one of his favorite rituals, this boy of mine.

People ask me how we let him go. How we untethered ourselves in order to give him a chance at a more independent life.

I never have a good answer for these questions. All I can say is every time it rains, I wonder if his own sky is metallic with clouds. And I hope he remembers his umbrella.

CHAPTER 1

Paper Cut Days: Autism and Grief

I notice a chill in the air.

I open the car door and begin loading in bags of groceries. I hear my name.

"Mrs. Cariello! I wanted to say hello."

A teenager boy with curly hair walks over to me. He's wearing a red sweatshirt.

We exchange pleasantries. He explains he worked with Jack last year. Side by side, they stood loading dishes into steam in a small local restaurant in town.

Chatting here, beneath the dusky sky, my breath catches a little.

> *His easy smile. His open, unguarded face. He is still. He holds my gaze.*
>
> *If it weren't for autism, this is who Jack might have been.*
>
> *Easy, open, unguarded, still.*

I often say autism is heartbreak by a thousand paper cuts.

Paper cuts sting. They are a distraction. They hurt just enough to make you stop, look up from what you are doing, and wonder for a moment if life could have gone another way.

It starts with Diagnosis Day.

No one is ever quite prepared for the day their child is first diagnosed. How could we be? It's like a splash of cold water on your face in the middle of winter.

I remember walking to the parking garage with eighteen-month-old Jack's hand in mine. It was November. He was wearing overalls and a blue jacket. It was as though time had stopped altogether, yet suddenly there was a clock strapped to my back.

Unfortunately, it's not the last time we experience the sensation of shock, disbelief, and perhaps despair. Diagnosis Day is just one of many, many days when you feel yourself come up short.

After Diagnosis Day comes The Telling. We have to make phone calls or send emails. We have to explain autism over and over again, before we even understand it ourselves. With each new conversation we falter just a little bit more. If only Hallmark made a card to help us announce this new normal—to describe the spectrum bell curve to aunts and uncles and neighbors. Until then, we bear the tiny stings upon our heart.

Over the years we watch other kids reach milestone ours struggle for—or may never reach at all. Driver's license, prom, high school graduation. And though we celebrate the triumphs, we quietly mourn our own loss. Paper cuts.

For me, the paper cuts change by the month, and the week—sometimes even by the day.

When he was about twelve, it was his glasses.

He has these wipes he uses for his glasses to keep them clean. He keeps a bunch of them in his pocket, and every twenty minutes or so he took one out, unwrapped it, and sniffed the damp cloth. Then he carefully removed his glasses, and wiped down each lens.

Twenty, thirty times a day he did this.

Watching him, I wanted to scream. No, that's not it. I wanted to cry. I wanted to cry for reasons I can't quite explain myself.

I wanted to cry because of the way autism takes a perfectly ordinary activity and transforms it into a full-fledged nightmare.

I wanted to cry because I will feel these small stinging cuts for the rest of my life.

As Jack gets older, I find the little heartbreaks come when I least expect it. I watch a boy his age dribble a ball on the sidewalk, all ease and athleticism, and my breath catches. I think of my tall son and wonder who he could have been, if autism didn't sometimes take charge of his arms and legs.

One time I noticed a girl looking at Jack when we were in the mall. I wasn't surprised. He's tall and handsome, and he was wearing his new coat and scarf. Then he hopped lightly in place. He flicked his fingers before his eyes and adjusted his glasses. She shifted her gaze to the floor and walked away.

Paper cut.

There is no formula for autism. But I have found there is a formula for healing from those tiny stings.

BE GENTLE WITH YOURSELF

On Paper Cut Days, be gentle with yourself. Order take-out for dinner—something comforting and delicious. When I called Joe from the parking garage to tell him the doctor said Jack had autism, he suggested pizza from our favorite place.

After dinner, sit on the couch. Use a nice, cozy blanket. Find something entertaining to watch.

Do not—no matter how much you feel tempted—*do not* immerse yourself in all things autism. I mean it. Don't go running to the library to reserve your book on neuroscience or brain disorders. Get off your phone and your laptop. Stop Googling things like *is there a cure for autism* and *how expensive are hyperbaric chambers?*

How do I know you're doing this? Because I was you. I am you.

I did all these things.

The same goes for television. No watching *Love on the Spectrum* or *The Good Doctor*. In time, you may find those sorts of shows interesting, but for now stick to what's purely entertaining.

AVOID BIG DECISIONS

Also, no big decisions on Paper Cut Days. Do not run out and cut your hair off or decide you need a big kitchen remodel.

No buying a horse because you heard horse therapy is the answer. No calling around for someone who can install a lap pool in your yard in the middle of December because you read somewhere that water helps kids with autism develop speech.

(I may have made that last one up.)

SUPPORT EACH OTHER

Avoid the temptation to pick a fight with your spouse. If you're like me, I often expect Joe to experience the same tiny hurts as I do. I've been known to get a teensy bit, uh, *irritated* when he doesn't. Let that go, and remember that we each grieve in different ways and at different times.

Likewise, if your spouse comes home, say, a little emotional after driving through town and noticing a bunch of teenagers doing ordinary teenager things, like playing pick-up basketball at the town courts or flirting with each other in packs at the ice cream place, don't say it's no big deal. Don't try to comfort him or her. Nod your head and offer a hug. Hold space for the ways in which we hurt.

LEAN INTO YOUR FEELINGS

Just sit. Place one hand just below your collarbone. This is the most comfortable position a human being can experience. Breathe. In through the nose and out through the mouth.

Lean into the feeling of loss and grief. Resist the urge to solve it.

TRY TO KEEP PERSPECTIVE

Try not to catastrophize, or leap to the worst-case scenario. Oh, I know! Catastrophizing is very fun. It's easy and somewhat rewarding. We think we're keeping ourselves safe by preparing ourselves for the worst, and if it doesn't happen, then all the better.

That's certainly one way to look at it, but it also keeps you firmly rooted in the negative. And when we stay in that space, it's very easy to lose sight of all the good that's happening all around you.

TRY THE HALT STRATEGY

I find the HALT strategy useful when I feel myself beginning to spiral a little. In those moments when you have trouble catching your breath, try asking yourself these questions:

Am I hungry?

Am I angry?

Am I lonely?

Am I tired?

Originally developed for recovering addicts, HALT identifies both physical stressors (hungry, tired) as well as emotional ones (angry and lonely). It also provides a brief interruption to the brain looping we often experience with anxiety—a moment to pause.

Once you identify any of the areas, circle back and address the easiest one. Have a snack, sit for a moment, text a friend, breathe.

BE REALISTIC

Last, on Paper Cut Days, consider what is possible.

For us, autism presented an opportunity—a chance to redesign our family in a way that challenged current societal norms yet felt right for us. In many ways it brought us back to the basics. Dinner at the table, faces aglow with candlelight. Sunday mornings in church, followed by a doughnut afterward.

You will find these things, too. Like a child sifting sand at the beach, you will discover precious seashells amongst the grit.

It's going to be hard.

It's going to be bumpy, messy, ordinary, thrilling, and triumphant.

It's also going to be okay.

It's going to be okay.

A life lived differently is not a life less lived.

In through the nose. Out through the mouth.

> *The teenage boy turns to go, all lanky stride and backward glance.*
>
> *Over his shoulder, his voice rings out like music. A Band-Aid for my spirit. A soothing balm for the sting.*
>
> *"Mrs. Cariello, I loved working with Jack. He worked so hard."*
>
> *I close my car door. I smile.*

CHAPTER 2

Autism and Food: How to Have Success at the Dinner Table

In the waning light I watch him set white plates out on placemats. Outside the window, flurries of snow drift lazily from the sky.

His face is earnest. He is concentrating on what comes next—forks, knives, napkins folded neatly into triangles.

I glance over at the menu board that hangs on the wall. Moments earlier, he'd carefully lined up the letters to spell tonight's meal. Beef tenderloin, mashed potatoes, green beans, garlic bread. It's a family favorite, one I reserve for Monday nights to celebrate the start of the week.

Dinnertime has always been an important cornerstone for our family. It's when we gather at the end of a long day. We catch up on news, tease one another, and share stories.

It is another way in which autism brought us back to the basics.

This doesn't mean it always came easily. Our time around the table was often fraught with tension and chaos.

Many times, Joe and I argued about what the kids should and shouldn't have to eat. Coming from wildly different backgrounds, this is our familial baggage at play. The youngest of six in a large Italian family, food is Joe's love language. Homemade pizza, pasta from scratch, Buffalo wings on the grill with extra blue cheese. Compared to his occasional cooking, my daily meals are prosaic—bland.

As a kid, he sat around the dinner table for hours on Sunday afternoon, cracking pistachio nuts and discarding the shells in a napkin arranged on the tablecloth for just this purpose. Music often played in the background. There was an ease to this tradition—comfort in their time together, accompanied by an abundance of food.

In contrast, when I was little mealtimes were often a battleground. My father was a disciplinarian with strict rules about finishing everything on your plate. I have more than one memory of sitting at the table long after everyone had finished, pushing lima beans around my plate. To this day I hate lima beans.

AUTISM AND FOOD: HOW TO HAVE SUCCESS AT THE DINNER TABLE

As an adult, I eat what I want, when I want. In other words, the moment I feel full, I stop eating. I could leave half a lobster to bring home or three bites of carrot cake. I loathe the sensation of being stuffed.

When we were newly dating, this drove Joe crazy. He eats what's in front of him, and quickly. And whereas his mother cooked extraordinary amounts of food, my mother cooked just enough portions for the people at the table. Once it was five, then we dwindled to four when my parents got divorced. Four pork chops, four baked potatoes, four ears of corn. I never remember eating leftovers.

There is no better stage for your marital drama about expectations around food than the dinner table. I'm sorry to say this, but it's true. With eyes as round as saucers watching you, you will argue about how many bites of broccoli is enough or whether or not the "clean plate club" promotes disordered eating.

We did, anyway.

It took some time for us to come to a mutual understanding about how we wanted our kids to eat, especially Jack.

Although Jack didn't have specific food aversions when he was little, he was what you would call a picky eater. He preferred what is known as the "beige" food category—pretzels, pancakes, chicken nuggets, French fries.

He refused anything with a lot of ingredients mixed together, like a casserole or lasagna. An occupational therapist once explained this was because he needed to sort through each different texture in his mouth—carrots, peas, potatoes—and make sense of each one before his brain could process the experience.

He dumped his plate on the floor. He dug his fork into the placemat. Over and over again, he jumped from his chair and ran in circles.

One night Joe and I looked at each other, completely frustrated. Jack was three. I was cleaning up milk that was dripping over the edge of the table. He was trying to feed Charlie and Joey while Jack hid under his chair.

It was time to make some changes.

TIMERS

The next night, we put a small wind-up timer on the table—the kind you might use while you're cooking. We set it for five minutes and told Jack he needed to sit until he heard it *ding*. I wasn't sure how much he understood, but after a few nights he started to connect the dots. He'd nibble at a few favorite foods on his plate—mashed potatoes, little bites of meatloaf—and then bolt from his seat when the timer sounded.

After a week we increased it to seven minutes. Then ten. Fifteen, twenty. Eventually, we didn't need it at all.

Running in circles. Spilled milk. One minute at a time. This is life alongside autism.

SCHOOL LUNCH

This may not be a popular opinion, but when Jack started first grade, we had him buy school lunch. Aside from the fact that I find packing school lunches to be its own form of torture, we thought there was value in having him participate in this daytime ritual. Standing in line, waiting his turn, sliding his tray along the counter—all were good opportunities to stretch his skill set.

I knew he would find something to eat. This was important to me. I knew our school had enough variety with their menu that he wouldn't go hungry, because the rest of the day would fall apart if he didn't get some food in him.

And, sitting alongside peers, he began to expand his palate a little more. Over the course of the year, the daily note in his folder mentioned he ate applesauce, spaghetti, egg salad.

Perhaps nothing to some, but monumental for us.

PORTIONS

Our developmental pediatrician suggested buying divided plates, the kind that come decorated with dragons or princesses or Thomas the Tank Engine. Then put the food out family-style—even dessert—and have everyone fill each section themselves.

They could eat in any order they liked—cookies first, green beans last—and have seconds of anything once every section was empty.

This took the fixation off dessert, for Jack and the rest of the kids. We didn't have to count bites of food. We didn't have to insist they finish their serving before getting a cookie or a bowl of ice cream.

MENU BOARD

When he was in elementary school Jack became interested in baking. After school, he'd choose a recipe. He'd assess the pantry and cabinets for ingredients. If we had what he needed, he pulled out the pans and began to work.

Watching him, I wondered if I could make him a part of the meal planning as well. He's always been good at organization.

I bought a really simple board that came with a bunch of plastic letters. I hung it on the wall and we called it the menu board. Every afternoon, Jack would line the letters up on the counter, and plug them into the black felt to spell out dinner.

Some of the more famous ones:

We're eating old food. (leftovers)

Dry ass turkey again. (two days after Thanksgiving)

Tonight we are eating something smelly. (crockpot fail)

He never disappoints, this boy of mine.

MAKE IT PRETTY

I have to be honest. I have never loved cooking.

But I do love making food look nice.

Pretty plates, tablecloths, placemats for each season—pumpkins and ghosts, evergreen and holly, bunnies with pink ears and cottontails.

When Jack went through the screaming, raging chaos that was puberty, we started lighting candles during dinner. As the flames flickered and the shadows played upon the ceiling, we breathed. It was all I could think of to do.

I guess you could say we made it less about the food. And when it was less about servings of vegetables and meat, we all relaxed. He relaxed. Our time around the table became much, much more than working with a picky eater. It became a sacred hour for our family.

AMNESTY NIGHT

A neighbor once told me about a game they played with their kids during dinner called Amnesty Night. Their kids could ask any question they wanted, or they could confess to anything without a consequence.

Now, I know what you're thinking. Ask anything? Make a confession with no repercussions?

I promise you, you won't regret it. We did it regularly.

They asked us how our parents met, about our heritage, and whether or not alpacas make good pets.

(They don't.)

The worst confession we heard was when Henry admitted he'd stolen Jack's watch to give to his sixth grade teacher, the beloved Mr. Brown.

We also had a couple of other games we played. When they were young, they loved reciting *Who Stole the Cookie from the Cookie Jar*. During the tween years *Table Talk* cards were really popular. Eventually, we stayed at the table for *Uno*, and

Heads-Up was a popular choice when someone had a new friend over. Or, come high school, girlfriends.

RESTAURANTS

Joe and I have always loved going out to eat. We liked trying new restaurants and exploring different kinds of cuisine. However, with each new addition to the family, it got harder and harder to do. Like many things in our world, autism only magnified the struggle.

Certain strategies were helpful when they were little. We kept what we called "go-bags" packed and ready by the door. Full of coloring books, mini-puzzles, and finger puppets, they were a great way to keep the kids busy while we waited for our food.

Also: crackers. Ask for them immediately upon sitting at the table. I cannot emphasize this enough.

Whenever we went out, we went early, and we chose restaurants that were kid friendly. Think chains, franchises, or small hometown cafes.

When he was younger Jack could be loud. He got out of his seat often. It was important to me that other people's meals weren't ruined or disrupted.

(This also includes Broadway shows, movies, and experiences like mini-golf or theme parks.)

A common family tradition is letting our kids choose where they want to celebrate their birthday. With five of them, you know we were spending at least one in a Japanese steakhouse—the kind with large hibachi tables where they create volcanoes out of onions and toss food into your mouth.

Let's just say Jack was not a fan. He made this obvious the time he crawled in on his hands and knees, shouting, "I hate. THESE PLACES."

The question came up: how do we respect his needs while at the same time honoring what the other kids wanted?

As it turned out, this question is not limited to only restaurant choices. Time and time again, we had to figure out ways to make circumstances comfortable for Jack so he could experience a family outing or tradition.

We had to meet him where he was. In the example of Japanese hibachi, this meant letting him bring headphones and his beloved music into the restaurant. We let him take breaks and walk into the lobby when he needed. We warned him when the onion was about to burst into flames. We didn't worry about what he ordered or how much he ate. Again, it was less about the food and more about him simply participating.

Through the years, restaurants also became a favorite of all our kids—especially Jack. Once he hit adolescence, it became another opportunity to stretch his skill set.

Up until that point, I usually ordered for him. But when he was around twelve we decided he should learn to look at the server, speak clearly, and ask for what he wanted to eat.

From there, we worked on how to put your napkin in your lap, make conversation, and even calculate the tip when the bill came.

DUALITY

I often say there is a duality that exists within Jack—his physical age and his emotional age. For as long as I can remember, there has been about a six-year difference between the two.

Perhaps you're wondering how this discrepancy relates to food. I think it does.

See, as our kids get older, we tend to loosen our grip a little on their nutritional choices, especially at social gatherings. The annual Christmas party is a time to let them overindulge on cookies and hot chocolate. A summer barbecue usually means a little extra ice cream and maybe another cheeseburger.

Once my kids turned ten or eleven, I let them decide for themselves what they wanted when we were at a social event. Yet I noticed I still tried to control Jack a little.

I realized this when we were at an annual Fourth of July party at our neighbors' house. Jack was twelve. There were the usual treats and desserts. I noticed, between swimming and asking people what kind of shampoo they used, he had never made a plate for himself, but instead was on his second brownie.

From my seat at the table, I started to admonish him—to remind him a burger first, then something sweet. But out of the corner of my eye, I noticed his older brother with a handful of M&Ms. I saw all the other kids racing around, eating ice cream and drinking soda.

It's important to know when to push, when to teach, and when to just let them soak up the sunshine and enjoy a little bit of childhood.

> *Standing at the stove, I turn back to my tall son. He is bent over the candles now, lighting each wick against the darkening night. He straightens. He admires the miniature flames—tiny toy soldiers dancing in orange. He looks at me. His face is aglow.*
>
> *"Mom. Everyone will be home soon."*

CHAPTER 3

How to Prepare for Family Gatherings

A yellow balloon glides across the counter. Three-year-old Joey grabs it with both hands. Next to him, Jack shrieks. He grabs for it. Both boys begin to squabble.

Joe's brow is furrowed, and his mouth set in a tight line. He takes the balloon away. Under the watchful eyes of thirty-something people, he leads Joey to the other room for a time-out. Jack continues to scream. My stomach sinks. I am so tired, my eyes itch.

Thanksgiving, 2006.

We are at my sister-in-law's for a big family gathering. We have two toddlers and a one-year-old. Beneath my long sweater baby number four is already beginning to show.

> *I know the hour-plus car ride home will be long. Joe and I will bicker, and then we'll be silent. We are so lost right now. I wish someone would tell me what to do—how to handle toddler tantrums and help Joe find his smile again.*
>
> *Out of the corner of my eye, I see my mother-in-law. She is watching me. She is watching us. Her eyes are kind. Concerned.*

It's been eighteen years since that Thanksgiving. Since then, we have endured many other terrible outings—barbecues gone wrong, family picnics where Jack dumped all the ice out of the cooler and stomped on the cubes, battles about how long we should stay at a party.

It took a while for us to find our groove, is what I'm trying to say. But, over time, we relied on a few strategies that proved to be helpful.

PREP, PREP, AND MORE PREP

Once you've accepted an invitation for a holiday brunch or a family reunion, set expectations ahead of time. Communicate them clearly to your hosts.

What does he need? What will you need?

HOW TO PREPARE FOR FAMILY GATHERINGS

If we were going somewhere that would be crowded, we knew Jack would need a quiet space to decompress if he got overwhelmed. A guest bedroom, the sewing room, or even a walk-in closet worked.

We also needed the ability to show up late and leave early without judgment or a lot of questions.

When he was in what I call the *wrecking ball* phase, where every knickknack, picture frame, and ornament was at risk for breaking, I suggested our hosts put away anything they didn't want broken. Because as hard as I tried to contain the whirling dervish that was my son, he was fast.

I found emails to be useful here. I could take a few minutes and craft a message to express my gratitude for the invitation, ask for a few things that might make the day more successful, and close with a sentiment of enthusiasm.

(This type of technique is often referred to as the Sandwich Method: Start with something nice, put the meat of the matter in the middle, and end with a few soft sentences.)

> Dear Aunt Mary,
>
> Thank you for the lovely invitation to your housewarming party!
>
> As you know, our son Jack is diagnosed with autism. He's making great progress at school, but parties can still be a challenge for him.

A small area where he can go to decompress is usually helpful. It doesn't have to be fancy—anywhere quiet will do!

We may be late, depending on his sleep schedule. If he gets overwhelmed throughout the afternoon, Joe or I may head home early with him. We don't want to be disruptive during what is sure to be a beautiful day.

If I remember correctly, you have a stunning collection of Faberge eggs. Jack doesn't quite understand the idea of decorative objects, so if you wouldn't mind putting them out of reach, I think it will bring us all peace of mind.

Again, thank you for including us in your special day! We can't wait to see your new home.

Love,
Carrie

Once you're done prepping your host, it's time to prep your kiddo. I always found it better to wait until just a few days before the party or event, otherwise he would perseverate on it a lot.

Social stories come in handy here as a way to explain what we *don't* do when we visit people's houses. We don't try to start their car (Jack did!), we don't roll around in their beds (he did this too!), and we don't poke holes in all the dinner rolls (yep!).

They are also a great way to lay out the expectations for behavior. We knock on the door, we wait for the host to answer, we greet them with a *hello*.

I always like give Jack an idea of the schedule—what time everything starts, when dinner will be served, and how long we plan to stay.

TOOLBOX OF ANSWERS

There's nothing like a family reunion to bring up uncomfortable topics.

Medication, behavior, food issues, how everyone is diagnosed with autism these days. At this point, I feel like we've heard it all.

During a graduation party, one guest asked me if perhaps more discipline would help with Jack's overarching anxiety, rather than medication.

The truth is, I don't like to defend myself on the spot. On the way home, I made a list of general, benign answers I could deliver quickly—ones that wouldn't invite a further line of questions.

> *We're working on it.* This is perhaps my favorite way to address comments aimed at behavior like swearing, touching all the food before he eats it, and the inevitable meltdown when the room buzzes with conversation.
>
> *I'm not sure.* I use this line when someone makes a suggestion or asks about Jack's future. Will he ever live on

his own? I'm not sure. Will he bag groceries for the rest of his life? I'm not sure. Will he ever have a relationship? I'm not sure.

Maybe we'll look into that. This is a great response to suggestions for essential oils, therapies you haven't heard of, and antiquated parenting strategies. Keep your face neutral and your tone of voice light. Do not engage.

It's easy to make a holiday gathering the battleground for defending your child and your choices surrounding a diagnosis. Trust me, this isn't the time to make your point. There will be other, gentler opportunities to help people understand your complicated life alongside autism.

For now, keep it short and sweet. Dig into your toolbox of answers, say your one-liner, and move along to the best part of any party. The buffet.

FOOD

Speaking of buffet, let's talk about food.

Food is often a major factor of every social gathering. But if you have a kid like Jack—one with texture issues and a sensitive olfactory system where certain smells really bother him—well, things can get tricky fast.

The goal is to have your kiddo eat. That's all. The day already has its own challenges. Routine has been disrupted. There are people who want to hug. This is not the time to experiment with a sensitive palate.

Get food in them. This can be a great big meal of their choice before you leave, or packing what they prefer to eat and bringing it with you.

Our kids already work so hard in these demanding social situations. Doing so on an empty stomach is that much harder.

Will people judge you? Absolutely.

Will Aunt Kristen complain that he didn't try her homemade chutney? Yes.

Will Uncle Leroy shake his head when you take out the frozen pizza and heat it in the microwave? For sure.

Refer to your toolbox of answers. *We're working on it.*

WELL RESOURCED

The worst reactions I have had where when I wasn't what a therapist once describe as *well resourced.*

Fed, rested, connected.

The morning of a big family gathering, try to move a little.

Sign up for a Turkey Trot. Walk a mile in the neighborhood. Spend some time on the Peloton. Run on the treadmill.

Think your big, ugly thoughts while you do this. Criticize Aunt Michelle in your head. Have a fake conversation with Uncle Leroy when he questions why you brought chicken nuggets on Christmas Eve. Leave it all here.

I know, I know. Who has time for this? You do. Announce to your family a few days ahead of time that you will need at least thirty minutes alone so you can be your best self for the rest of the day.

Afterward, have a good breakfast. Don't skimp on calories. Don't save room for shrimp cocktail or turkey. Eat eggs with sourdough toast. Use lots of butter because butter is important.

This is what's called building margins into your day. This means being realistic about how long it will be before you get some decent food in you after you wrangle kids out of the car and into the house and hug the aunts and take off coats.

Move.

Eat.

Breathe.

Oh, and on the way out the door, kiss your spouse.

This brings me to my next topic: *Don't turn on each other.*

DON'T TURN ON EACH OTHER

If I'm being honest, Joe and I don't, uh, always *agree* when we're trying to manage our kids in front of people. We lose our good feelings for one another.

It usually starts with a passive aggressive comment.

Remember, you love each other.

This may be your hardest work yet.

SEPARATE CARS

This is perhaps the most important part of this chapter. Separate cars are a must, at least in the beginning.

I know the inclination is to arrive as a family. That's what all the other families do. You want to be like all the other families.

You are not like all the other families. This might make you sad and resentful, but it's true.

You are a family who needs an exit strategy. A family who has to take the needs of siblings into account—siblings who enjoy jumping into a pool at a Fourth of July barbecue and banging pots on New Year's Eve.

Joe and I started doing this when Jack was around eight. Prior to that, we drove in one car, and Joe and I almost always wound up arguing about how long to stay. I guess you could say it's our difference in parenting.

Joe likes to stretch Jack just a little further each time. As much I as do too, I don't like to do it under the watchful eye of family and friends. I don't like to be on display when I try to calm him down or get him into his jacket.

We learned over time that the other kids like to stay a little later on Thanksgiving or the annual fish dinner on Christmas Eve. (Joe's Italian, remember?)

One time, Joe's car was in for inspection on the same day as a birthday party for his niece. Since we needed to drive together, we agreed ahead of time on when we would likely need to leave the party. If separate cars aren't possible for you, this sort of planning is essential.

NO

"No" is a complete sentence. So is "Not this year." Also "We're not ready for it yet."

All are acceptable answers when it comes to invitations to barbecues, water parks, weddings, or birthday parties.

No doesn't mean *never*. In most cases it just means this isn't the time. Perhaps your kiddo is in the grips of anxiety. Perhaps you are trying new medication or there is a behavior you're trying to curb, like elopement (running away every chance he or she gets).

BE THE HOST

I know, I know. This sounds crazy. Make a Thanksgiving turkey while your three-year-old with autism insists on smearing the walls with soap? (Jack did that.)

Invite your closest friends and family on Christmas Eve while your five-year-old with autism tries to flush the toilet 5398 times an hour? (Jack also did that.)

Hear me out, though.

We moved to New Hampshire in the spring of 2007, when Jack was just shy of three. We didn't know anyone in our neighborhood. And, although he was in preschool, I felt like very few people got to meet him or understand what autism looked like in our family.

When Halloween rolled around, I decided we should hold a small parade on our street. The idea was to have all the little kids in costume walk to music and end up at our house for pizza before it was time to trick-or-treat.

We printed up fliers and pushing a double stroller with my daughter in a Baby Bjorn on my chest, we trundled up to all the mailboxes and delivered them.

It was a huge success, and a tradition we kept for well over a decade.

As the kids grew older it was less about the parade and more about darting around our yard in the dwindling light. As dusk drew close, nearly sixty people gathered inside for pictures and snacks every year.

My intention behind this was twofold. First, I wanted people to see Jack in his home environment—the space where he's most comfortable. I wanted everyone to get to know him when he was calm and regulated. It was the perfect amount of time—about two hours from when people arrived until the mass exodus for trick-or-treating at 6:00. He could mingle as he liked and take a break in his room if he needed one.

Second, it was a great way to stretch Jack's theory of mind as the role of host. What might our guests like to eat or drink? What kind of playlist would work for background music?

What is the right way to open the door and greet someone? Can you smile and say, "Welcome!" Can you offer a drink or a slice of pizza?

And when the clock strikes 6:00 on the dot, can you resist the urge to fling open the door and shout, "It is TIME. For everyone TO LEAVE." (Yes, Jack also did that.)

WHAT CAN YOU LET GO OF?

You've done all you can think of to do. Social stories, emails, rehearsed responses.

A moment before your guests arrive, or you step out of the car to walk into a party, place one hand on your chest—right below your collarbone. This is the most comfortable position a human can experience.

Breathe.

What can you let go of today?

If you're hosting, can you forgo perfection in the name of paper plates and a store-bought cake?

Can you resist the urge to roll your eyes when your partner forgets to pack juice boxes?

Most importantly, can you let others meet your beautiful child halfway?

Can you let them bond on their terms?

Can you let them figure one another out without standing in the way?

Can you see that there are others in the room who might be able to soften your sharper moments with their own kind of tenderness?

> *My mother-in-law got up from her seat. She walked over the corner and picked Joey up in her arms. Sitting back in her chair, she cradled him close to her.*
>
> *"Enough," she said quietly to the room. "That's enough for today."*
>
> *The balloon floated limply to the floor.*

REFLECTION POINT

Think back to your most successful family outing (using your own definition of what "success" looks like!) What made it work?

CHAPTER 4

Autism Siblings

We dropped Jack off at his program in July. A few weeks later, I took the other four kids to walk around a little town we love. On the way home, stopped for dinner at our favorite burger place.

We brought our burgers and fries to a patio overlooking the street. Conversation moved lightly from one topic to another—the upcoming school year, whether we should stop for ice cream, which friends were coming over later that night.

"You know guys," I confessed. "Sometimes I worry I wasn't there enough for all of you. You know, when you were younger. I worry autism took up too much of my time."

Everyone got quiet. Four faces turned in my direction. Inside each one, I saw every infant, every toddler, every kindergartener they once were.

I held my breath.

GLASS KIDS

This is a popular term floating around the Internet to describe the brothers and sisters who live alongside a diagnosed child. It refers to the way they are often unseen, or invisible. Their needs go unnoticed.

I first heard this a few years ago, when all five of my kids were teenagers. It made my breath catch.

I know, I always say worry less about the attention you pay your kids, and more about the attention you give your marriage. I still believe that.

But with five children I knew I had to make sure each one felt seen and heard. I knew we needed to stretch ourselves to meet their needs as well.

People often ask me how we decided to have more children after Jack was diagnosed. I wish I could give an astute, practical answer, but the truth is we were pretty careless. The day after we learned Jack was autistic, I learned I was pregnant again. With my fourth child.

While we were not very adept at family planning, I will say several doctors told us that the best thing we could give Jack was a big family. That being said, it is a topic I don't like to advise families about, as I know autism can show up more than once.

In fact, although none of our other kids are diagnosed in our house, I compare autism to a bowl full of brightly colored jelly beans. From social anxiety to rigidity, each of my kids has reached into the bowl and grabbed a piece of candy for themselves. Jack, on the other hand, reached in and grabbed two fistfuls (at least).

I will say there was tremendous benefit in Jack having siblings. For one thing, he had role models for speech, language, and social situations. He also had a built-in group around him at home, which I think help eased some of the loneliness he may have experienced at school.

Since they were so close in age, Joe and I essentially moved the kids throughout the day as a unit—until they got older, they ate at the same time, took baths and showers at the same time, and went to bed at the same time.

Mostly though, Jack couldn't be in charge. A bit on the, uh, *bossy* side, having siblings meant that Jack learned to compromise, or go with the flow. He couldn't always be the one to pick what movie we were going to watch or where to go for ice cream. You might say a larger family provides a built-in instruction manual for turn-taking.

There comes a time when younger siblings pass their older one in development or milestones. In our house we call this *leapfrogging.* Every time it happens I imagine a small green frog leaping over the first in line.

WHAT IS THE RELATIONSHIP LIKE BETWEEN JACK AND HIS SIBLINGS?

This is one of the questions I am most asked. There is no way to answer it quickly.

I usually start off my saying my kids are very, very different. At times it's hard to believe they came from the same parents or were raised in the same house.

Joseph

My oldest son, Joseph, is twenty. He's tall and fit, with green eyes and light brown hair. He is thirteen months older than Jack, and currently pursuing a degree in finance.

From the time he could sit up, Jack chased his older brother.

Charlie

Our third son, Charlie, is a senior in high school. He's the only one of our kids with Joe's dark hair and brown eyes. Committed to playing baseball in college, he'll be the next to leave the nest.

Rose

Rose, our only girl, is sixteen. She was the latest one to leap-frog over her older brother—this time with her driver's license. At six foot one, she rows for the crew team.

Three years younger than her brother, I have always likened Rose to the proverbial canary in the mine—the songbirds miners used to test the air quality before they descended into the shafts themselves. Once the music stopped, they quickly resuscitated the canaries using special cages they carried with them.

She has always been greatly attuned to his energy. When she was in elementary school, she noticed he didn't sit with anyone on the bus.

When sixth grade's storm hit him like a blizzard, she braided long strands of yarn together and offered them to him.

"Jackie," she said, calling him by the nickname only she used, "use these when you feel yourself getting mad. Pull on them hard." He carried them everywhere he went.

To this day she has a quiet way about her—more prone to observation than interjection. The day we dropped him off at his program, she stood quietly to one side of the parking lot. Tears streamed down her face.

Henry

Henry, the youngest child—the fifth and final, as we like to say—is a freshman in high school. Already on track to be the tallest in the family, he towers over Joe and I already.

I'm not trying to suggest our house existed in perfect

harmony, because it certainly did not. We've had our share of sibling rivalry over everything—from who brings in the garbage cans to who is better in school. But these are some of the principles that have helped.

FAIRNESS

There were also protests about fairness, particularly when it came to Jack and homework, since he stopped having to do it sixth grade. My answer was always the same: There's no such thing as fair, and everyone in our house is expected to do what they're capable of doing.

OPENNESS

Don't let autism be a secret in your home. Talk about it openly. Acknowledge the many gifts it brings to the world. We always reminded Jack that, whether it was birthdays, the lyrics to a song, or what year a movie was made, he had the best memory of anyone we've ever known.

At the same time, once he fully understood he had a diagnosis and what it meant, we often talked about how everyone in life has mountains to climb. He was not alone in working toward particular goals.

MAKING TIME

When our kids were young, we made a point every month to spend a little extra time with them on the day they were born. I know, this sounds confusing. Here's an example: my daughter Rose was born on July 21st, 2007. So on the 21st of every month, either Joe or I did something with her—we walked in the neighborhood, baked some cookies together, or, as she got older, went to the coffee shop for her favorite latte.

> *Did I have guilt about them each not getting enough attention? Of course I did. Over the years I went to bed worrying I didn't spend enough time with them, or I wasn't patient enough, or was spread too thin.*
>
> *I chalked it to typical maternal worry, but beneath my ribcage a nagging worry persisted. Was I doing it all wrong?*
>
> *Back at the table, with our burgers and fries, I watched their faces carefully. Rose reached for the ketchup. The sunlight glinted off her hair.*
>
> *"Mom," Charlie said. "That's not how we remember it."*
>
> *One by one, they chimed in, offering their favorite memories in my direction like the silkiest flower.*
>
> *Scooby-Doo marathons in the playroom, breakfast*

at Grandma's, the time we missed the flight to Turks & Caicos. The year the Christmas tree fell over, the best places to hide Easter eggs, the first time we brought Wolfie home as a puppy.

Together, they laughed and remembered.

Sitting outside on a summer evening, I looked at each of my kids.

I don't know about glass, I thought to myself as the sun made its quiet descent across the sky.

I only know about the boy who walked off the mound after a springtime game, drove to the store, and bought his brother a birthday present.

I only know about the canary in the mine—the tender girl who calibrates her nervous system alongside her brother—and the strongest pieces of yarn.

The oldest brother who keeps one eye on the future and the other looking over his shoulder.

And the youngest, the fifth, the final, the son who stretches his brother without breaking him.

Building a family is messy.

Collect your flowers. They make the loveliest bouquet.

CHAPTER 5

Strategies for Money and Budgeting

After twenty-five years of marriage, Joe and I still don't always see eye-to-eye on the big stuff.

In fact, just last night we argued about money again. Jack's debit card was declined. He was trying to order food from Uber Eats. French fries and a frozen Pepsi. He called Joe and me over and over again to talk about it. We checked the account. There was money in it. We assured him it was some kind of blip with the app. Still, he was panicked. He was scared he wouldn't have any money. He doesn't understand why it happened.

After the final phone call last night, Joe and I sat on opposite sides of the couch. Our voices climbed. He thinks he's ordering too much delivery. He should use his money for other things. I think it's something a lot of college kids do. He is sticking to his budget.

> *As is often the case, a disagreement about take-out bloomed into something larger, the way a small spill on the rug becomes a stain. We went to bed angry. This is an Autism Marriage. It is real and raw. We alternate. One worries, the other hopes. All the while, our ribcages vibrate with thoughts of the future. What will happen when we're no longer here? Who will make sure he doesn't spend all of his money or get scammed out of his savings? Who will remind him to keep his wallet in his pocket when he walks down the street?*

As I write this chapter, Jack is in his second year at his college program. Money and budgeting continue to be a challenge for him.

After a few months of him relentlessly asking me to Venmo him money, I slid the budget piece over to Joe. He's better at saying no than I am, if I'm being honest. He and Jack came up with a weekly amount of spending money, and Joe adds it into Jack's account every Monday. It is more than enough to cover the small things he wants to do or buy, and most outings are paid for by the program itself.

Part of the problem is Jack's overall naivete about money in general. He has a hard time understanding the concept of a lease, or a mortgage, or a bank loan. It's difficult for him to imagine that when you take cash from the ATM, it's also being subtracted from your checking or savings account.

It's further complicated by the fact that we live in a mostly cashless society. The tangible nature of currency is missing, especially for someone as literal as Jack.

At the same time he has tremendous anxiety surrounding it. He feels like he will run out of money at any moment. The result of this is him asking us over and over again to "reimburse" him.

And he loves to shop! Amazon, Target, Walmart. His tastes aren't expensive necessarily, but he is an organizer by nature, so he likes to stockpile things like soap and shampoo. He is also easily persuaded, so if he sees a commercial announcing that cold and flu season is upon us, his immediate reaction is to buy a lot of cough drops and Vicks Vaporub.

It's important to note that this was one of the reasons we obtained guardianship once Jack turned eighteen. As guardians, we have the ability to protect him financially if someone convinces him to transfer money or buy something on their behalf.

Unfortunately, Joe and I don't always see eye-to-eye on the topic of Jack's spending.

I think Joe feels the pressure of providing for Jack for the rest of our lives. He wants him to understand money and create good habits.

I, on the other hand, feel like Jack doesn't long for a lifestyle of luxury. Simple things make him happy. A trip to the movies or a waterpark. Ice cream on a summer afternoon. A humidifier for the winter months and take-out delivered by DoorDash.

The concept of finances is one that forces me to consider the lens: Is this autism? Or just a college kid trying to figure out how to manage his money for the first time? After all, we know plenty of college kids who blow through their entire savings in one semester.

Let's just say Jack isn't as far along in this area as we hoped. However, there were a few things we, mostly Joe, did for years that I think helped.

RECEIPTS

Joe is better at this than I am. Whenever they went to the hardware store or grocery shopping, he'd go over the receipt with Jack. What were the most expensive items? What was the cost per pound for grapes? Was the gallon of ice cream worth $3.99?

(Jack's answer: Yes.)

It was an attempt to get Jack to understand that money has value. It's not an unlimited resource and we have to make choices on where to spend it.

TIPS AND COSTCO

Whenever we ate out, Joe would show the bill to the kids and ask them to help calculate the tip.

Although a seemingly simple exercise, it helped started the conversation about service and compensation.

In a similar attempt to connect the dots about the value of money, Joe would take all the kids to Costco once a month. With several cards loaded up, he'd ask them to guess how much everything might cost, *Price is Right* style. The one closest without going over won.

Joe does love Costco.

BANK VISITS

When Jack was in high school, he got a job washing dishes for a local restaurant. As soon as he got his very first paycheck, Joe started bringing him to the bank. They'd go on Saturday mornings, often stopping at Dunkin' Donuts for breakfast first.

Once there, Joe guided him through the line until they reached the teller. He showed him how to fill out the deposit slip. He helped him add the numbers in the ledger and with a pen, modeled how to sign his name.

They sat with a bank employee at one point and filled out the paperwork for a debit card. Joe took Jack to a few stores so they could practice how to use it—everything from inserting it into the machine at the cash register to signing his name on a receipt.

KEEP IT SAFE

Joe constantly reminded Jack—and all of our kids—how to keep their money safe. One year for Christmas he bought them all wallets.

Never take a wad of cash out in front of a bunch of people. Always keep your bills folded neatly and organized by dollar amount. Don't leave your debit card out where people can see it. Don't let anyone hover over your shoulder while you're at the ATM.

WHEN ALL ELSE FAILS

When all else fails and we can't talk through a concept and help him understand, we make it visual.

It's been difficult to communicate to Jack what parts of his lifestyle we will continue to pay for, such as haircuts and his medication, and which parts he is expected to manage, like Door Dash and tickets to the movies.

After reassuring him for the zillionth time that we will pay for his medicine every month, I decided to create a graphic so he would refer to it whenever he felt anxious. I used an umbrella, with the items beneath it the ones he needs to pay for, and the raindrops outside of it the costs we cover.

> *This morning I sat at my desk. The sky was gray. The clouds looked like they had something to say, if only I could read the mist.*
>
> *My phone buzzed on the charger. It was Jack. He told me he called the bank. He explained the problem. He filled out the paperwork and ordered a new card.*
>
> *He did this because of Joe.*
>
> *He did this because every Saturday morning he brought him to the bank.*
>
> *He showed him how to make a deposit, sign his name, and check his balance.*
>
> *He taught him how to ask for what he needs and reach for all that is rightfully his.*
>
> *I don't know if we'll ever stop arguing. I don't know if we'll ever see things from the same point of view.*

> *I do know this. No one loves this boy more than this man.*

CHAPTER 6

Puberty

Standing at the window, I watched Joe's car head out of the driveway. He turned and made a left up the street. Bracing myself, I turned back to Jack.

"MOVIE! I go to the MOVIE! No, no NO!" He screamed. He bangs both fists on the floor.

"Jack, no movies today. You can't go, remember? You have to write an apology."

"NO NO NO they all get to go I want to go!"

"I know, buddy. I know you do. But we don't kick teachers. You have to apologize."

That week, Jack had kicked his sixth grade math teacher in the leg. It was the third time I had to pick him up from school. Day after day, I parked in the lot. I walked past the parents waiting in the carpool line.

> *I retrieved my son from the classroom or the principal's office, and I walked back out while everyone watched. Each time, I hung my head in shame.*
>
> *He was twelve. His behavior was out of control. Puberty had created a perfect storm of chaos, and we had no idea what to do.*
>
> *After a lot of discussion, Joe and I agreed. He wouldn't be allowed to go to the movies with the other kids unless he apologized.*
>
> *All weekend, we negotiated. We asked him to write a few words down. At one point, I took out a piece of paper and a pencil. I left them on the counter and urged him to write one sentence to his teacher. One sentence, and he could go to the movies.*
>
> *The paper sat there, blank.*

People often ask me what it's like to raise a teenager with autism.

I tell them the truth, of course. I tell them Jack's experience with adolescence has been nothing short of wonderful. He has soared through the changing landscape of his body without incident. His hormones have remained fairly consistent.

I'm sorry, I couldn't resist. Every once in a while, it's nice to write our own narrative, isn't it?

Ever since Jack was a toddler, I've wanted a crystal ball to see into his future.

I guess I just wanted to know how it all turned out—I think a lot of special-needs parents feel this way. We could relax a little if we had some idea of what was in store.

In my mind's eye, I imagined different versions of Jack as he got older—waving from the bus on the first day of kindergarten, maybe, or running on the beach in his bathing suit. Every now and again, I would squint into my proverbial ball, and pictured such niceties as story time at the library, and middle school graduation.

I knew there would be work, of course. I knew the waves and the running and the library would result from careful planning and social stories. Still, I imagined all the scenarios in which Jack would advance through his young life. Occasionally my brain would flit to the idea of him as an adult, but I always shrank back as though I'd come too close to a flame.

Never once, however, in all this prediction and forecasting, did I imagine what it would be like when he became an adolescent. I can't explain why. It's as though my mind couldn't conceive the idea that this chubby little boy would eventually grow hair on his face and sprout pimples like an alfalfa field.

I never considered what it would be like to have a son whose body forged ahead into manhood, while his emotional spirit stuck close to Disney movies and chocolate-chip pancakes on Sunday mornings.

It doesn't really matter anyway. Looking back, I don't think there is a crystal ball in the whole world that could have helped me prepare for the storm that is autism and puberty.

I mean, at best, adolescence is a complicated time for a regular old neurotypical kid. Take one who struggles with crushing anxiety, delayed social skills, and executive functioning, add some hormones and a little underarm hair, and things can really go off the rails.

Adolescence is described as the period of time when a child enters puberty and begins the process of transforming into an adult. For males, this typically happens between ages thirteen and eighteen.

According to the *Encyclopedia Britannica*, "Young persons experience numerous physical and social changes, often making it difficult for them to know how to behave. During puberty young bodies grow stronger and are infused with hormones that stimulate desires appropriate to ensuring the perpetuation of the species. Ultimately acting on those desires impels individuals to pursue the tasks of earning a living and having a family."[1]

---

1   Encyclopaedia Britannica (2024) Puberty. www.britannica.com/science/puberty.

PUBERTY

I read that description when I was trying to figure out how to explain puberty to Jack. I did not find it especially helpful.

Nothing had prepared me for this point in motherhood—not a single article, or book, or conversation.

Nothing prepared me for how I'd have to jump in the car after the dreaded phone call, the one reporting that my son Jack was out of control, he wasn't safe, and I needed to pick him up and bring him home.

I'd walk into the school, past a line of students sitting on the hallway floor. The first time this happened, I thought they were all in trouble, or waiting for something special to start.

Then I noticed a few teachers, with walkie-talkies. And that's when I realized; they had to clear the room so no one was hurt because my son was out of control and he was not making good *choices* and trying to throw computers.

My son, my gentle giant, my glasses-wearer, my chocolate-cake-baker.

He was hurting too, I didn't know how or why, but he was coming apart before my eyes.

I was ushered into an empty classroom by a man with kind eyes, and I found my son. Most times, he was crumpled on the floor, gulping for air.

UNDERSTANDING THE TEENAGE YEARS

Hormones. Anxiety. A shifting social landscape. In the teenage years, these factors create the perfect storm. For Jack, the storm descended when he was twelve. Sixth grade was an absolute disaster.

Hormones

We all have hormones.

A hormone is nothing more than a chemical released into our bloodstream, designed to send a message to other parts of our body.

For example, the hormones in my forty-nine-year-old, perimenopausal body are telling my brain to eat a lot of sourdough bread and wear pants with elastic waistbands.

But teenage hormones are next level. They are fierce. As the chemicals responsible for physical growth and sexual development, they cause mood swings, irritability, and impulsive behavior.

Anxiety

Jack was initially hit with anxiety when he was in first grade. It crushed him like a ton of bricks. After attempting a few other measures, we eventually turned to medication. And while it didn't take the anxiety away completely, the medicine smoothed out the edges throughout elementary school.

Sixth grade brought on a new wave of it altogether. First, he stopped sleeping—all night long I heard him toss and turn in bed. His sheets and blankets were crumpled in a ball in the morning. His body was always in motion—either picking at his cuticles or pacing the periphery of the room. He reverted to looping and scripting.

We consulted with the pediatrician and decided to increase the dosage. It helped for a bit, but was not a complete fix.

The social landscape

I just love the phrase *social landscape*. It sounds lofty, and important, and smart. It suggests a backdrop where friends frolic and laugh, calling to mind easy days and ice cream cones.

In reality, social landscape is the terrain upon which relationships are developed and sustained.

Unfortunately, during middle school and adolescence, this terrain can be rocky. It shifts without warning, leaving one stranded, and often alone.

Most kids adapt to the changes after a while. Maybe they drift to new group of friends, or join a club they find interesting.

Jack is not most kids. He is not known for his flexibility, or ability to *drift*, if you will. He has never in his life belonged to a club, no matter how many times we encouraged it.

"Hey, Jack, how about the chess club? They meet every—"

"No."

"Well, we could try swimm—"

"Nothing. For me."

An occupational therapist once told me younger children with autism are drawn to the company of girls, because at that stage of development girls will handle all the communicating. In Jack's case, this was true—he had a cluster of little girls who talked for him, sat with him at lunch, and navigated the complicated land that is the American playground with him.

The same therapist went on to explain that as kids develop into tweens—those lovely pre-adolescent years between ages ten and thirteen—girls resort to non-verbal social clues, and kids like Jack are left in the dust of their eye rolls and shoulder shrugs.

> *Jack made two friends that year–two sixth grade boys. They met on the playground and played made-up games. They call themselves "The Group."*

For someone who has been friendless for most of his life, this was a very big step.

Yet, like most things in Jack's life, the things that bring him joy also cause him stress. Trying to untangle the mysterious web of social interactions was no different.

For most of the fall, the three of them stuck together. But in the spring, there was a newcomer, a twelve-year-old boy who also wanted to meet on the playground and play made-up games and be considered a part of "The Group." And Jack felt threatened—jealous.

"They are for MAGNETS TOGETHER," he screamed at me one afternoon as he threw his backpack down on the floor, his voice rising on the last two words.

"Okay buddy, calm down. What happened?"

"They are mine. Mine friends. Not HIS."

Night after night was like this—a perpetual looping ring of confusion and despair.

The academic curriculum also changed. He struggled to complete the simplest of assignments. Math especially overwhelmed him, as the focus turned to language-based word problems rather than computing black and white numbers.

He refused to do homework. Every afternoon turned into a battleground at the kitchen table, as I alternated between pleading and scolding. He couldn't sit for longer than ten minutes at a time. Many times, defeated, I told him to pack it up—the worksheets and folders and books—and put it away for the night.

He barely ate dinner. He raged and stomped through the house. I could hear him tossing and turning in bed, just as I tossed and turned in my own.

One morning he came to me and said, "For my ear. Is wrong."

I'd noticed he'd been picking behind his earlobe with his finger in a nervous, twitchy way. When I looked, I saw he had rubbed the skin raw. It felt like he was trying to erase himself.

It's difficult to capture the heartache that is watching your child descend this way, while you stand helplessly to the side.

In late spring, I called our developmental pediatrician. She'd known Jack since he was in first grade, when anxiety first descended like a ton of bricks. She was familiar with our story, as well as puberty in adolescents with autism.

"Carrie, tell me what's been going on."

I squeezed my eyes shut. I was sitting in my car in the parking lot of the mall. The sky looked smudged and dirty, as though a child had drawn the gray clouds with a crayon.

I kept my eyes closed, and I tried to explain all the things I'd been ashamed to say out loud for six months.

I explained that I didn't know how it got **so bad** with Jack. I told her how he says terrible, terrible things, like our family has changed for him and he is a loser and everything is so stupid. He hates me, he hates us, he hates himself.

I tried to tell her how his need for routine intensified. Constantly he asked what we're doing one week, one month, one year from now.

His body was always in motion. It was like watching autism control his arms and legs, the way a puppeteer manipulates the strings on a marionette.

All he wanted to do was sit on the computer and rearrange songs into long playlists, or watch the same movie trailer a dozen times. And when I took the computer away, he just wandered around listlessly, alternating between rage and despair. He jumped up and down and clenched his fists and cried.

He called me the worst names he could think of—he accused me of being a drug dealer and a bastard and, one time, a hermaphrodite—and even though I don't think he even knew what any of them mean, it still hurt.

Yet when I asked for more; to try and understand why, why the playlists, why the trailers and the rage and the names, he shut down altogether.

"Jack, what do you mean, you are a loser?"

"Nothing. What are we doing Friday. December 30th."

I tried to put into words what it feels like to mother to have a child who gives almost nothing in return— not a hug, not a smile, not a kiss. I would have given nearly anything for a smile.

Or the way he developed his own private language that sounded like a series of beeps and grunts, and when he wasn't beeping and grunting, he was talking about some kind of conspiracy theory—something about being framed and taking revenge.

I couldn't get him to do anything. He wouldn't sit with me to read a book. Once a beloved activity, he refused to bake anymore. The cookbooks sat unopened on the counter. His favorite pans—the one shaped like a heart, another one with the square bottom—went untouched in the cabinet.

When he wasn't angry, he was vacant. Lost to us. At night he hovered in the doorway of the family room. We invited him to sit on the couch and watch TV with us, but he remained in the shadows, skittish and unsure.

"I know, I know," the doctor said softly when I paused for a breath. "Carrie, he's a cat right now, not a dog."

Hearing her say this, I felt like I had looked underneath the couch, and in the middle of all the Lego and discarded socks, I'd finally found the last piece of a long, complicated jigsaw puzzle. It was dusty, and one corner was a little bent, but it fit perfectly.

"For now, he just needs to know you are there. He will come back when he's ready, I promise."

It felt impossible. It felt as though this season of our life would stretch out interminably. As so often the case with autism, I couldn't see the end.

Right before we hung up, she reminded me gently, "Carrie, remember. Cat, not a dog."

At his most panicked, frantic moment, he talked about knives and hurting himself. We hid them once he went to bed at night. We were terrified.

We asked him what was wrong. "Nothing. Everything."

We met with his team. "Jack seems to be struggling quite a bit with his peers."

In the evening I made phone calls to mothers, when Jack had lashed out at their sons and daughters. "I am terribly sorry about what happened today. My son is in a bad place, and we are working on it."

At night, Joe and I turned options over and over—was this a reaction to medication? Were the academics too demanding?

In the end, I believe it all it came down to hormones, loneliness, and loss.

Neurotypical kids have a hard time explaining the sensation of a hormonal mood, or irritability. For Jack, it's nearly impossible for him to describe.

Every night, Joe and I turned options over and over—was this just puberty? Or another uptick in his ever-present anxiety? Were the academics too demanding? How much longer could it last?

Desperate, we turned to a neuropsychologist for an evaluation. Week after week, Jack and I trudged through the slushy parking lot and up one floor of a medical office, where he sat with a young dark-haired doctor for various tests. Some involved problem-solving concepts. Others, a test of his working memory, emotional well-being, and language comprehension.

In life and motherhood, some details are easily forgotten. Others are hazy at first. They take a while to come into focus,

Yet meeting with the doctor to learn the results of her time with Jack is still razor sharp. From the sound of a car starting in the parking lot below us, to the panic spreading through my ribcage, I remember it all.

"Well," she said gently, "He has some issues with working memory."

I looked at Joe and back at her. I nodded my head. I'd heard of working memory.

"Picture our working memory to be this entire table," she continued.

She spread her hands over the wood surface. "We have all this space to arrange our ideas." She fanned some of her papers out to demonstrate.

"We can organize the things we're thinking about. We can put some things here," she said, gesturing to the right.

"And other things here." She moved a folder to the left.

"But Jack, well, his working memory is more like this." She made a small circle with her hands in the empty corner of the table. "He doesn't really have as much."

He doesn't really have much working memory. His table is empty. Like a gust of wind on a rainy day, autism swept all his cerebral papers and folders and sticky notes to the floor.

"It's as if we all have a filing cabinet in our minds,"

she continued, stepping inside of my reverie. "It's where we store all of the information we absorb throughout the day. Jack has his own kind of filing system, but it's hard to know what that's like. His information is, well, it seems complicated."

I uncrossed my legs and then crossed them again. I glanced at Joe in the chair next to me. He seemed to be squinting at something on the wall.

"His cognitive thinking is quite impaired. He's probably less than two percent of his peers at this point, but it's difficult to tell because his anxiety gets in the way."

"Based on his scores, his reading comprehension is close to that of a first grader."

"While I was testing him, he often said things like he feels like a loser—that he feels alone."

"When I showed him a math problem, he would tell me he's dumb at math, he can't do it."

I struggled to stay focused. I pictured Jack in first grade. He was so cute. I had bought him a red backpack for the first day of school. His name was stitched across the front in white letters.

> *"You see, he doesn't process language the same way we do. For Jack, listening to people talk all day is like you or I sitting in a French class, except we don't speak French. He only understands bits and pieces here and there."*
>
> *I remember feeling a powerful wave of regret and fear, like nausea. The room was hot.*
>
> *"I do think he's probably a little depressed."*

It was during this period in our autism journey that we became very concerned for Jack's safety.

You see, there is a side of autism no one likes to talk about—one that includes thoughts of self-harm, injurious behavior, and suicidal ideation.

In the height of his panic, Jack struggled with depression coupled with severe anxiety. He mentioned knives and death. He became fascinated with celebrities who had committed suicide. In particular, he seemed obsessed with Michael Jackson—how he died and his funeral.

Yet at the same time, there was a detachment to these preoccupations. It was almost as though he was an observer to his own thought process, if that makes sense. He never talked about directly hurting himself, but still, we were terrified. Day after day, we watched over him. Night after night, we took the block of knives off the counter and hid them away. We didn't know what else to do.

Deregulation during car rides also became a very real problem. At twelve, Jack was nearly five foot nine inches tall. (For reference, I am also five foot nine inches tall.) Getting him in and out of the car when he was deregulated was challenging. Once I convinced him to buckle in, usually with the promise that he could control the radio, I had to make sure he was calm enough so I could actually drive. Several times I was concerned he might open the door while we were on the highway.

MAKE THE OVERT, COVERT

When it comes to Jack, it's also important to figure out *when* to give him information—if you tell him about something too early, and his anxiety has time to kick into gear, he'll only obsess and worry and bite his cuticles until they bleed. Timing is everything.

That's where the puberty talk got tricky. So, we did what all good parents do, and we avoided it until the last possible second. Maybe a little bit too late, as it happens.

We had to do what we always do, which is to make the covert, overt—or take what might seem obvious to us, and name if for him.

"Jack, your body looks uncomfortable right now. What does it feel like?"

"I am not. In my rightness."

Then, we had to normalize it for him.

"Buddy, everyone feels this way around this age. It is completely normal."

SAFE LANDING

Much of the time—then, and now—Jack lives in what we call *fight or flight* mode.

Fight or flight is a state of acute stress, when the body's nervous system becomes activated according to real, or perceived, fear. Those with anxiety, like my son, are triggered quickly and easily.

He can only match the highest regulatory system in the room. This means it was important for me to stay calm for him—to not let myself get swept up in his riptide of rage.

This was especially hard when his behavior spiraled. He swore. He called us names. He stomped around and ripped his homework to shreds.

What did I do? What magical methods did I employ to

transform myself into a peaceful mother with an angelic smile?

Sadly, after *much* trial and error, I landed on some helpful breathing strategies I learned in yoga. I also started to just leave the room when he got elevated, as a way to give us both a break.

Every day after school that terrible year, Jack would walk in the door, throw his backpack down, and go straight upstairs. Fully clothed, he'd climb into my bathtub and huddle there. He never turned the water on—he simply closed his eyes and cocooned inside the porcelain.

The first few times he did this, it made me feel edgy. What was this new routine? After a week or so, I realized he was working on regulating himself after a long day. He needed a small space to feel emotionally safe. I decided to take my cues from him.

During the day I bought special treats at the grocery store—avocados, a certain kind of pretzels he liked, parmesan cheese for spaghetti.

In the morning I smoothed his crumpled sheets and made his bed just the way he liked it, with the pillows stacked neatly and his beloved stuffed bunny nestled amongst them.

Schedule became important. I tried not to surprise him with last-minute appointments or errands. I wanted him to relax into our family's routine as much as possible. I thought after the unpredictability that was school at that time, the least we could do was keep a consistent rhythm at home. Dinner, television, shower, bed.

Weekends were for breathing, not rehashing all that went wrong at school.

It seems trivial, to make sure dinner is on the table around the same time, and that we follow a regular bedtime routine. It's hard to imagine a neatly made bed could shore the rising tide of autism's rage and chaos.

And yet did. It provided a framework into which Jack could relax, and recharge.

Nothing resolved overnight. But after a few weeks, I sensed an ease in him—in all of us.

THE *WHY* BEHIND THE *WHAT*

You can't punish a child at 4:00 in the afternoon for something they did at lunchtime. You can't create a teaching moment after dinner if your child couldn't sit for circle time in the morning.

Oh, we tried it! We took away his beloved *Scooby-Doo* episodes at night. Many afternoons, I admonished him all the way home for his behavior. Thinking about it now makes me sick to my stomach.

It wasn't working. Kids like Jack don't connect the dots. When he got elevated in school, he didn't remember the quiet night before without television and attempt to behave. This was a regulation issue, not behavioral.

We had to figure out the *why*—the trigger or reason—behind the *what*. In this instance, the behavior was our *what*—kicking, lashing out, swearing.

I learned that a tantrum has a goal. More cookies, another movie, a later bedtime. A meltdown, on the other hand, is a response to the environment; the lights are too bright, the music is too loud, the shirt is too scratchy.

This was a critical piece of information for me. How would I categorize his outbursts at school? Did he have a goal in mind? Did he want to get out of work or come home early? Not really. He wanted to stay with the other kids and finish the day. So it had to be a reaction to the environment.

As anyone who has ever stepped inside a school during the day knows, it's loud in there. The hallways are buzzing between periods. The cafeteria is noisy. The gym is full of kids bouncing balls of the floor and the backboard.

On top of that, you can immediately smell the food being prepared for lunch.

Once I considered all the ways in which Jack's five senses were immediately engaged the moment he stepped foot inside the school, I could better understand why he remained so deregulated throughout the day.

And while we couldn't exactly remove all the stimulus, it gave us the chance to consider building more sensory breaks into his day—a quiet space in the counselor's office, or a chance to walk down the hallways alone.

MORAL COMPASS

Every single time the school called me to pick Jack up, I felt like a failure.

I'd walk past all the parents in the carpool lane, waiting to pick up their well-behaved kids, and my face burned with shame. I wondered what I was doing wrong—why my son had such bad behavior.

We tie our moral compass to our kids' behavior. This is a normal inclination. Oftentimes, it feels like a reflection of our value system, our parenting, our own ego.

When it comes to autism and behavior, it is not.

I needed to take some time to fully understand this. His behavior wasn't the result of poor parenting. It was simply the combination of many factors creating a storm within my son. Once I separated myself out of the equation, I could fully focus on solutions—once again, figure out the *why* behind the *what*.

Eventually, we moved him out of public school. I was devastated, as was he. But—puberty or not—we needed to slow things down a little, and make his world smaller, where he could cocoon, feel safe, and start to learn once more.

LOVE HIM THROUGH IT

The third time the school called me, I was so frustrated, I wanted to throw the phone against the wall.

Desperately, I wanted to believe he understood. I wanted to believe he knew the relationship between behavior and outcome—the familiar narrative of if I do A, then B will happen.

He didn't.

I had to love him through it. This was very hard work.

I don't mean butterflies-rainbows-cliché kind of love. I mean the gritty, raw, tender kind. The kind that requires us to listen, hear, try, and hurt.

When my thoughts veered toward frustration, I tried to choose a gentle voice. When my heart leaned toward admonishing, I reminded him he was good. Inside and out, I started to root for him.

After all, I've never once heard a mother say she looked back on her life and wished she yelled more. I've never heard anyone say they were glad they traded *Scooby-Doo* for a seat in a circle.

In this difficult season, I decided I would simply love him as best I could.

Looking back, I'm scared there are moments when I forgot.

On the afternoons when I had to pick him up, I'd walk slowly toward him, as though he was a rare bird who would fly off into the clouds if I moved too fast. When I reached him, he'd stand up. I folded him in my mother-wings, careful, so careful, not to wrap too tight.

He laid his head on my shoulder and we swayed together lightly like leaves in the soft breeze. He wept, and I wept, too. I wept because of him and for him and with him.

"Hold on, buddy," I whispered. "Hold on to me. Spring is coming."

The paper sits on the table. It is still blank. The afternoon light fades in the windows. We have spent the afternoon in gridlock over an apology.

I look at my tearstained boy, huddled in a ball on the floor. This isn't working. Nothing we're doing is working. We are stuck.

"Jack, buddy. Come here. Come sit with me."

He lifts his head. He gets up from the floor. He walks toward me slowly. He sits down next to me. For a moment, he lets me stroke his hair.

As my fingertips graze his head, I feel less stuck. I feel a lightness I haven't felt in nearly a year.

I will love him through this.

It could work.

CHAPTER 7

How to Give the Sex Talk

It started with a conversation at the dinner table one night. After all the other kids left to do homework or watch TV, he lingered for a little longer.

"Is it fun," he asked with his eyes narrowed.

"Uh, well," I said. "It's like–"

"Yes," Joe interrupted.

Jack got up from the table, crossed his arms, and marched away. "You are. Disgusting."

The next afternoon he started in on me as soon as he stepped off the bus.

"So you secretly had THE SEX without us knowing."

"I guess. Come on, let's talk about this inside. I made cookies for snack!"

But he was not interested in redirection. "When was the last time you did it."

"I don't remember."

"What time do you do it. The sex. 2:00 am? 3:00 am? In the AFTERNOON?"

"I'm not sure."

"Do you do it to music."

"Not really."

"Does it take like fifteen minutes. Or an hour."

"It depends."

"Do you have to hug the person."

"Yes."

"Are you allowed to do it. With your clothes on."

"Not really."

> *"It sounds like the lamest. Thing ever."*
>
> *"Uh huh."*
>
> *He stood with his hand on the doorknob. "If I have to do it. I will keep my clothes on."*
>
> *"Okay, that sounds like a good plan, Jack-a-boo."*

When my oldest son went through puberty, his voice changed gradually. I'd hear him somewhere in the house and think for a moment that my husband was home from work early.

Jack's voice changed overnight. One day he was talking to me in a high, sweet tone about *Toy Story*. The next day he sounded like he was barking from the bottom of a cave. I think he even startled himself.

His changing body also caused him quite a bit of concern. He was particularly rattled about the idea of body hair. One time we took all the kids to SeaWorld. We stood in line waiting to see the dolphins when Jack noticed a man wearing a tank top. He turned back to us and announced at the top of his lungs, "For ME. I will SHAVE. The PIT HAIR."

Many parents I know complain their teenagers don't wash their face enough, or they emit body odor like steam from a rank ship. You can practically see it, I've been told.

We have always been lucky when it comes to hygiene. According to the order imposed upon him by autism, Jack begins every day with a shower. He is fastidious when it comes to keeping his nails trimmed, and his hair neat, and he loves nothing more than a good skincare routine. Although this fastidiousness can border on obsessive compulsiveness, I'll take what I can get. Picking your battles, I have learned, is paramount when it comes to teenagers.

As I mentioned, timing is everything with Jack. I think we started to warn him when he was about eleven that he was going to experience a few changes in his body. It gave him just enough time to formulate a plan for pubic hair, but not so much time that he could stockpile shaving cream.

We always had a feeling he was going to be tall. While the Cariello side is not known for great height, my father and my brother are both quite tall. Every doctor who ever met Jack mentioned he was going to be tall one day. So we told him that over the next few years, his body was going to grow and grow, and he needed good food and lots of exercise to stay healthy. In his young mind, this advice translated into something that sounds like, "Eat many pancakes a day and refuse to get off the couch without a fight."

Battle-picking. I cannot stress it enough.

What we did not anticipate, however, were his reactions to growing pains. You know the pain in your legs that can accompany large growth spurts? I had them as a kid, and I remember them well. They hurt, and sometimes they kept me up at night.

Jack, on the other hand, demanded to be transported to the hospital by ambulance. He insisted trips to urgent care were needed. He pretended he couldn't walk. This is very consistent with his catastrophic attitude and anxiety. It's also a little bit entertaining, if I am being honest.

Once again, make the covert overt.

This was advice a psychologist once gave me. It means take all the nuanced, subtle parts of life and make them obvious.

Sadly, it also applies to explaining sex.

When it came to the Sex Talk, delicate euphemisms weren't enough to help Jack understand it all.

Listen, I'm not embarrassed about sex. It is natural. It is ordinary. It is normal, and in many cases it's brought forth beautiful, annoying, messy, loud, impatient children.

We didn't tell him everything, of course. I was afraid his head might actually explode—that the neurons and synapses and whatever parts of his cerebral cortex responsible for processing information might start to smoke and catch fire.

I mean, we're talking about a boy who would rather bump into the kitchen counter to avoid brushing his arm against mine. A boy who has never, ever even one time by accident or when he was dozing off to sleep or crying because he hurt himself, reached for me with both arms or kissed my cheek goodnight.

Autism is oftentimes without boundaries. This means if Jack can touch it, ask it, say it, use it, type on it, or otherwise consume it, he will. He doesn't seem to possess the same instincts as most when it comes to keeping his hands and his ideas to himself. This includes leftovers in the refrigerator, my favorite towel, and his father's socks.

Add that to a complete lack of filter, and you've got a real party on your hands.

In other words, whatever we told him about sex and babies and puberty, I knew the cashier in Walgreens would hear about it too.

I am very hard to embarrass. I consider this my best quality.

My husband Joe, on the other hand, well, let's just say when it comes to the kids, he handles the practical questions about taxes and changing the oil in the car, and I handle things like sexual intercourse and prophylactics.

That being said, I hail from an age where you figured this stuff out on your own. Maybe a friend of yours had HBO, or an older sibling with a little advanced knowledge about anatomy. You never once thought to ask your parents. You did not, under any circumstances, walk up to your mother while she was scrambling some eggs and inquire about sperm. It just wasn't done, is what I'm telling you.

In fact, the only practical advice I ever remember my mother giving me in this area was, "Once you *do it*, you can never go back to only holding hands." I think I was seventeen at the time. I might have been getting ready for the prom.

Fast-forward about three decades, and here I am, standing at the stove making breakfast. Three out of my five kids are teenagers. They ask me whatever crosses their mind.

BE HONEST BUT SELECTIVE WHEN ANSWERING QUESTIONS

I am a firm believer that kids don't need to know everything all the time. Raising a child on the spectrum has only bolstered my confidence in this area. So, yes, I aim to provide a comfortable environment where my children can come to me and tell me everything and ask whatever is on their sweet, gentle minds.

I am willing to answer any question that's lobbed my way, but I don't answer anything pertaining to me, personally, as in, "How many times have you and Daddy done it?"

ANSWER THE QUESTION THAT IS ASKED

In the same vein, I answer the question that is asked. This has served me very well. For example, if a child asks me what a Fallopian tube is, I explain it is the tube where the egg moves from the ovary into the uterus. I do not take this opportunity to launch into an entire explanation of conception and pregnancy and ejaculation. If the conversation takes us there, fine, but I believe in following their lead.

This may strike you as lazy, but I truly believe kids ask questions because they are ready to know the answers. Nothing is scarier to a budding teenager then learning about intercourse and all that accompanies it. I like to pace myself.

KEEP IT SIMPLE

So how did we explain sex to Jack? Well, very carefully, of course. And when I say *we*, I mean most of the words were coming out of my mouth, while Joe hovered in another room and listened to me field questions like, "How long. Does THE SEX take."

You have to remember, even though Jack's voice lowered about six hundred octaves during puberty, his delivery remained the same—think zero inflection, Arnold Schwarzenegger style.

I kept it simple. I used social stories and books to help illustrate. I normalized his fears about touching another human being.

ALLOW TIME FOR FOLLOW-UP

Mostly, I just made myself available to him. He processes information very differently than most, and I knew answering one question might spur three more in the next day or so.

Kids like Jack are often drawn to the taboo—topics most consider off limits. Sex was no exception. It was as if he needed to exhaust every aspect of the subject before he could move on to something else.

HYGIENE: SET EXPECTATIONS

Like the Sex Talk, it's important to set expectations in a way that is concrete—black and white.

I know some parents struggle with their teenagers when it comes to hygiene. We never had much trouble with Jack in that sense. I'm not sure if this is because he has obsessive compulsive disorder, happens to *love* any and all products and skincare routines, or just pure luck. I imagine it's a combination of all three.

We did set what we call a Standard of Care in our house. Shower once a day. Brush teeth in the morning and before bed, at the minimum. Hair combed and presentable. Deodorant must be used before school.

Back at the dinner table that night, I steeled myself for more questions. But Jack seemed content to lose himself in everyone else's chatter about their own day. One by one, each sibling left the table to finish homework or watch TV.

Jack lingered for a moment. I could tell something was on his mind.

"I guess I'll wait. Until I fall in love. Before sex."

CHAPTER 8

Autism, Dating, and Social Media

"Jack, hold on, I can't understand you!" Joe said frantically into the phone. "Please, calm down."

April 8th, 2022. It was almost midnight. Nearly a year into his program, Jack had called Joe. He was screaming.

Joe had come upstairs to wake me up, and I stood next to him in the living room. My heart was pounding. It took a few minutes to understand what was happening. Slowly, punctuated by Jack's shouting and Joe's attempts to calm him, the story emerged.

A few weeks earlier, Jack had connected online with someone he thought was a peer. He used a popular dating site. After trading messages back and forth, they arranged to meet in person at an abandoned building on a Sunday night.

Jack walked there from where he lives. Instead of a teenager, two young men were waiting when Jack arrived. They convinced him to get into their car, drive to an ATM, and attempt to take out money.

They drove to a small convenience store around the corner and stayed in the car while he went inside with his debit card. For whatever reason, the card didn't work. When Jack returned to the car, they agreed to bring him back to the meeting spot. Jack got out of the car, and it was only after they drove away that he realized his wallet was missing. At that point, he called the police.

When it came to sending Jack to live away from us, this was Joe's very worst fear—that he would be persuaded and eventually harmed.

"DAD! I will FIND THEM! I will SLASH THEIR TIRES."

"Jack!" Joe said, "Breathe."

"I HATE THEM!"

"Okay, Jack, please put the officer on now."

> *There was a rustling sound as Jack handed the phone to the officer standing nearby.*
>
> *"Hello, Officer? You're with my son Jack. He has autism."*
>
> *"Yes, thank you. I figured that out when I met Jack."*
>
> *Climbing back into bed several hours later, our hearts were broken.*
>
> *Where did we go wrong?*

We gave our oldest son a phone when he turned sixteen and got his driver's license. We figured that was a pretty good rule and planned to extend it to the other four. Prior to that, they had iPod Touches and, in my middle son Charlie's case, a flip phone.

The fly in this proverbial ointment, of course, was that Jack didn't get a driver's license. Joe and I debated when to give him his own phone, and eventually decided, in the spirit of fairness, he should get one on his sixteenth birthday too.

The problem became management. Like many kids with autism, Jack is particularly drawn to technology. I wouldn't say he is big into video games, but just the general overload of information that having the virtual world at your fingertips offers.

The other problem was—and I will try to put this delicately—the kind of websites I knew he would visit and how to manage his access.

I've mentioned the duality that often exists in kids like Jack—their physical age and their emotional age.

It's not commonly discussed, but the truth is people on the spectrum experience the same physical urges for intimacy as their neurotypical peers. Many long for a similar connection and relationships. For many years, Jack's asked us if he'll ever fall in love or get married.

About six months into his program, Jack asked if he could have social media. We agreed to an Instagram account with privacy settings. We laid some ground rules about what was appropriate to post—stay away from politics, sexual jokes, or anything that could be considered inflammatory.

A few months after he started using Instagram, he came to us with another request. He wanted to use online dating apps to meet someone. We said no way. In fact, I think those were my exact words. *No way!* We didn't think he was emotionally mature enough to handle it.

Our reaction also reveals our own age—Joe and I didn't date in a time when people met online. You met the good old-fashioned way, at parties or on campus or through work. If you were really daring, you went on a blind date that your cousin or your roommate set up for you. We kept telling Jack that's not how relationships work; you don't meet through a screen.

But today, people do. We had to wrap our own minds around this idea.

VIRTUAL STRANGERS

From the experience I've just described, we learned that once kids like Jack—or any teenager or young adult, really—connect with someone online, they no longer consider them a stranger. Even if they've only exchanged messages, they feel a sense of familiarity before they even meet in person.

This was really important for me to realize, so we could caution him that who he talks to through messaging and on a screen may not be an actual representation of the person.

Kids like Jack are often easily persuaded. A literal thinker, he believes what people tell him and who they say they are. It's difficult to teach suspicion or wariness.

TOOLBOX—A WAY OUT

Looking back, Joe and I realized we made a terrible error in parenting Jack. Since he spent much of his childhood in the company of adults, we never prepared him for the possibility of an uncomfortable situation the way we did with our other kids.

In fact, we did the opposite. Because Jack's anxiety often prevented him from committing to social events, once he did, we insisted he honor his obligation, whether it was a birthday party or board game night at school.

On the other hand, we talked to our other four kids about what to do if they were in a situation they didn't feel comfortable with—whether it was a party where there was drinking, or a high school football game, or a sleepover. If there was a red flag of any kind, we would help them leave.

We agreed on three concrete things to say in such a circumstance:

My dad would be really mad if he knew I was here.

My mom just called, she said I need to go home now.

I don't feel well at all.

We also agreed on a *safe word*, one they could use when they called or texted us, and we would pick them up immediately—no questions asked.

After that night in April, we knew we needed to do the same with Jack—and we needed to take it one step further and have him come up with the responses himself, so he could say them confidently if the time came.

In the days following the incident, Jack admitted he felt something was off when he first arrived at the meeting spot. He said he only expected one person, not two men. He didn't like the way their car looked or how they were behaving. He just didn't know how to make an exit.

In what we now call his "toolbox" for when something feels wrong, Jack came up with the following:

I need to call my father now.

I want to leave now.

I'm late for (class, a meeting, dinner).

When sitting down with your kiddo to come up with their list, be sure to keep the responses short and direct, so it's easy to deliver them under stress.

SOCIAL STORY

I know, I know, we thought we were done with social stories once our kids got out of elementary school, didn't we? Yet there are times I still find them useful in helping Jack understand an unfamiliar situation.

An abandoned warehouse. His phone battery was on two percent. He hadn't told a single person where he was going or when he'd be back. It's the stuff they use in horror movies.

I thought he knew better, to be honest. I never considered Jack to be a risk taker. At the very least, he is fastidious about making sure his phone is charged.

But I think the excitement of meeting someone—and the chemical feedback that accompanied it—overruled any sense of caution he may have had. Coupled with our insistence that he *not* seek out company this way, it was the perfect storm of secrecy and recklessness.

In this case, the social story is twofold, as we needed to explain what he should do when meeting someone for the first time, as well as what his new contact or friend *shouldn't* do.

Make the overt covert. (Yes, this phrase shows up a lot in my life—and this book!) But never assume your kiddo understands even the most basic safety tenets when it comes to online dating and social media. It's better to overprepare here.

Again, now that he's older, we had him participate in making the list. Neuroscience tells us the ideas we arrive at on our own are the ones that stick in our minds the most. This is what we came up with together:

Before you meet someone in person for the first time:

- Charge your phone to 100 percent.

- Choose a popular public place where there will be people. A coffee shop, a park, Ben & Jerry's.

- Tell at least three people where you are going and when you expect to be back.

- Remember your "toolbox" if something feels off when you get there.

- If the person doesn't resemble their online photo, leave immediately.

- Never get into a car.

When you meet for the first time, the other person should never:

- Ask you for money.

- Ask you to buy something for them.

- Suggest a sexual encounter or going back to where they live.

LAW ENFORCEMENT

A few minutes into the call, Joe told Jack to put the police officer on the phone. Joe explained that this was his son and he had autism. The officer said he already understood that. We could hear him trying to soothe Jack in the background.

Luckily, the officer involved with this incident had been

trained to understand signs of autism. But that may not always be the case.

It's important to expose our kids to law enforcement early and often, so they feel comfortable around men and women in uniform. Have them talk to the resource office at the school, and go to open houses at the police and fire department. We'd done all of that with Jack.

Yet we never thought to explain how he should behave if he ever needed to call the police. Frankly, he was so deregulated, I was terrified the officer would misunderstand his intentions and arrest him.

Afterward, we talked to Jack about specific ways to interact with law enforcement. We came up with this short list:

- Take very deep breaths to remain calm.

- Explain that you are diagnosed with autism.

- Keep your voice down.

- Never make threats or speak about violence.

For weeks, I catastrophized about this incident. I'd wake up at 4:00 am and think of everything that could have gone wrong. He could have been abused or abducted, or worse. He could have gone missing.

Joe, on the other hand, decided to focus on this as a learning opportunity. Despite it being one of his biggest worries when Jack left, he was calm about the whole thing. He kept reminding me that yes, it could have had a terrible—possibly tragic—ending, but it didn't. We got a second chance.

We opted not to pursue the case any further or try to find the two men. The officer suggested it was a basic cash grab—they were simply in it for a chance to get money quickly. Overall, there wasn't enough evidence to track them down as they deleted the profile from the website. We thought it was best to keep Jack moving forward here, as his anxiety can often keep him in a space where he ruminates on things in the past.

As for me, after about a month I started to use what I call Whole Brain Thinking to move on—when I started to think of every worst-case scenario, I allowed myself to thoroughly consider each one. Then, once I finished with that list, I forced myself to think of all that went right.

Two days later, I was on a call with Jack. He admitted

there were several red flags he noticed when he approached the meeting spot, especially when two men stepped out instead of the individual he was expecting.

"Mom, looking back, there were things that made me uncomfortable. I just wasn't sure what to do."

"I know, buddy. I'm sorry."

CHAPTER 9

Raising a Whole Child

> *"What should I ask for in our IEP meeting next week?"*
>
> *Through the screen, her face was earnest. I could feel her determination radiating from her. I'd been on the Zoom call with a group of parents for nearly an hour. Hers was one of the last questions.*
>
> *"Do you think he needs more speech therapy?"*
>
> *Desperately, I wanted to give her the answer she longed to hear, that yes, extra time with the speech therapist and more goals added to the already long list would transform her little boy.*
>
> *"What helped Jack get to this point?"*

I wish I could say there was a formula to this autism journey—if you do A, B will follow. The truth is, there wasn't one particular therapy or service that helped get Jack to where he is today.

I also once pinned all my hopes on the conference room and the sheaf of papers that I clutched in my hands. But it doesn't work that way.

Our first IEP meeting was in Buffalo, New York. Prior to that, I had never heard the words *Individualized Education Plan* in my entire life. I assumed everyone had the same plan for the same day at school. I never knew about things like accommodations.

It's important to remember you are trying to raise a whole child.

A child who can forgive, and order in a restaurant, and cheer someone up after a bad day.

One who can sit in church, or his brother's baseball game, or through brunch at a fancy-ish restaurant.

A whole child doesn't spring out of a conference table or leap off of a page covered in black and white goals.

You and your partner each have a role to play in your new familial landscape. You have to let him play it, even if it's different than yours.

In other words, resist becoming The Person.

I did pretty well for the first year I was a mother. Our oldest son Joey was born and, for the most part, my husband Joe and I handled the responsibility of taking care of a new baby fairly equally.

I didn't care how he swaddled him, or what he which outfit he chose, or whether he used the blue pacifier with the duck on it or the green one with the frog when he fussed.

*Then Jack was born. He was a little, uh, **unusual** right from the beginning. He never looked at us, he never slept, and he cried all the time. Both Joe and I saw it. We were both worried.*

We exchanged uneasy glances on the couch late at night while we took turns rocking and soothing and walking our angry, mysterious baby.

Then he was diagnosed with autism. And things changed.

We didn't sit together on the couch as much. We didn't exchange the glances, and we didn't take turns soothing. I think this was because, overnight, I became The Person.

After the diagnosis, I was the only person who could

feed Jack his mashed bananas that he spit right back out at me. Only I could rock him to sleep so he would wake up twenty minutes later screaming. I knew just what kind of juice he preferred.

I threw myself headfirst into specialists. I read articles. I researched therapy. I was frantic, and yet I thought I was the only one who understood him.

There I sat, on my island of invented expertise, like a carping queen in her ivory castle.

I took Jack right along with me. We looked around, and we looked at each other. We looked across a wide, deep spectrum moat that separated us and we saw all the other people out there, having fun and laughing and sitting in the sun.

This was not good; for me, for Jack, or for my marriage.

See, when you are the only one who can do everything and you do it perfectly and you sneer and roll your eyes when someone else tries to step in and help, then you will wind up doing every single thing yourself. And this will make you mad. A little sad too, but mostly mad.

*Because, if you are anything like me, you will blame your husband since clearly, he is very lazy. He is maybe even a little bit stupid because he doesn't understand that the special diaper cream **must** go on every time this little hiney gets changed and if the bananas have any lumps then it won't work. And the green bowl is really best because the bottom is flatter.*

You blame and blame and maybe you feel resentful. Resentment is like a tiny seed that plants itself in your heart and your mind. Except instead of blossoming into a beautiful, silky flower, it grows into an ugly weed at a time when you most need colorful petals.

This was me.

I bought the special diaper cream because I obviously cared about our son the most.

I mashed the bananas in the green bowl.

I sneered. I rolled my eyes.

And then we almost got divorced.

I am not kidding about this.

RESPECT THOSE AROUND YOU

Back then, I thought it all mattered so much. I thought that if I didn't do everything exactly right then Jack wouldn't *outgrow his autism* and our life would be miserable. That's what the voices in my head told me, anyway.

Well, we were pretty miserable, but it wasn't because of his autism. It was because I was trying to control my life's unfamiliar landscape through ridiculous details.

It was because Joe's opinion ceased to matter.

It was because I was alone and angry and sad on my island, and I didn't even know how I got there.

People like me, we use smugness and sneering and bananas to protect a small inner light. This light, it flickers like a candle on a windy day.

The wind is trying to control our vulnerability and make it disappear. Vulnerability is scary. It makes us feel weak and cold and alone. It makes us feel defenseless.

We build a wobbly fortress around our candle out of sticks and stones and green plastic bowls. We hide it from the wind, and the world, and maybe even ourselves.

With my marriage crumbling before me, one stick at a time, I dismantled my fortress. I tried to weed out the resentment.

The truth is, Joe, when it comes to this unusual boy of ours, Joe is much better at many things than I am.

He always shows him the receipt when they go grocery shopping so Jack can see that apples were on sale but the grapes were more expensive than usual.

And when Jack is tired, or he has a headache, it is his father he seeks. He stretches his long body on top of Joe's, and closes his eyes.

He is the gain to my loss—the ultimate balance sheet of marriage and parenting.

DON'T BE THE PERSON: ACCEPT SUPPORT

I can't lie. Every now and again the old voice in my head starts to whisper, and I fight the urge to become The Person again. I read the latest research on autism and begin to panic, or I worry Joe won't remember to give Jack his medicine when I'm out with my book club and maybe I should write down a little reminder.

He always remembers.

Do me a favor. Take a moment today and look in the mirror. Look yourself right in right in the eye. Are you The Person? Are you standing in the way of a loving, messy, unpredictable relationship because you have marooned yourself on an ivory island?

TEACHING AND LOVING

The wind will stop blowing, I promise. You will stand straight and tall and honest in the still, tranquil air. Nothing bad will happen to any of you. It is in the quiet space of light where life is lived best. Together, you will move away from the stuffy conference room and into the sunshine.

From there, teach this child everything you can think of to teach.

Teach him to bring the garbage cans in at night and to throw a load of towels in the wash.

Teach him how to dial 9-1-1 in an emergency and the way out of the house in case of a fire.

And on your hardest days, when autism has stolen the very air you breathe, love him through it.

What if all we had to do was love our children?

Love them through their mistakes, their poor judgment, their outbursts.

Their vulnerabilities. Their moods. Their highs and lows.

For eighteen years, doctors and therapists have told me what to do.

Use social stories, try medication, redirect his obsessions.

No one ever told me to simply love him.

Love the way his hair smells after a bath.

Love the way his chubby fingers grip a pencil.

Love how carefully he stacks his pillows at bedtime.

Love him through it.

Love him through this diagnosis that will follow him forever, like ants at a picnic.

Love him when anxiety clutches his spirit and smile.

Love him through his veneer of shame and embarrassment.

What if we loved our kids through spilled milk, bad report cards, middle school?

I don't mean a butterflies-rainbows-cliché kind of love. I mean the gritty, raw, tender kind.

The kind that requires us to listen, hear, try, and hurt.

MAKE THEM SAFE

What if we made our home the safest of spaces?

What if, during puberty, we bought special treats at the grocery store, and made beds smooth with blankets, and lit candles during dinner?

It could work.

It could help our budding teens exhale. It could help smooth the jagged edges of their hormones and their acne and their furiously changing bodies.

Inside they are wilting flowers upon a fragile vine.

Inside, they need us even as they stubbornly push us away.

This boy Jack has lived under a magnifying glass for his entire life.

For as long as I can remember, his very existence has been quantified in terms of how many hours he slept, how he sat in his chair, how often he made eye contact.

What if we measured it by smiles?

LOVE RATHER THAN DISCIPLINE

Jack has autism. He also has severe anxiety, and obsessive compulsive disorder.

You can't discipline any of this out of him. I know because I tried.

I tried telling him to stop being afraid of the wind chill factor. It didn't work.

I tried taking his beloved nightly *Scooby-Doo* episodes away when he couldn't sit for circle time at school. It didn't work.

We need to love them through it.

One time the school called. Jack was in sixth grade—a time when anxiety had taken a deep hold of him and manifested itself in his behavior. In other words, he kicked, screamed, cried, and bit his way through the day.

When we hung up, I was so frustrated, so worried, so aggravated, so tired, so lost, I wanted to jump up and down and scream.

I wanted to believe he understood. I wanted to believe he knew the relationship between behavior and outcome—the familiar narrative of if I do A, then B will happen.

He didn't.

In the instant before I threw my phone against the wall, I realized.

I have to love him through it.

This would be my hardest work yet.

When my heart leans toward admonishing, I'll remind him he is enough.

When my thoughts veer toward frustration, I'll choose a gentle voice.

Inside and out, I will root for him.

After all, I've never once heard a mother say she looked back on her life and wished she yelled more.

I've never heard anyone say they were glad they traded *Scooby-Doo* for a seat in a circle.

Today, I will love him through this.

> *Looking back, I'm scared there are moments when I forgot.*
>
> *When I saw the diagnosis before the boy.*

When I reached for the towel before smelling his bathtime scent.

When I told him to stop, stop worrying and pacing.

Earnest Mama. Today, forget the IEP table. Set the magnifying glass aside.

Who knows, maybe you'll find the light no one else can find.

You are enough.

We are enough.

It's never really about the bananas.

Chocolate-chip cookies. That's what Jack bakes when his dad has a bad day.

CHAPTER 10

Tips for Marriage

> *"How do you find time to give enough attention to all five of your kids?"* It was hard to read her expression, given the tiny box that framed her face over Zoom. She wore glasses, perhaps a ponytail.
>
> I leaned back in my chair. I'd been presenting to a mom's group for nearly an hour. When she said five kids, ducklings came to mind—all yellow feathers and jaunty walk.
>
> Looking back at the screen, my words tumbled over themselves before I gave them any real thought.
>
> *"Worry less about the attention you give your kids, and more about the attention you give your marriage."*

I hadn't planned to say anything like this. I planned to tell her about all the ways we tried to make sure each child was seen and heard—how we nurtured their individual personalities and hoped they weren't eclipsed by the demands of the autism spectrum.

And while all of that is true, at the heart of it all was marriage.

Joe and I met when I was nineteen and he was twenty. We were both juniors in college.

We dated for two years before we got engaged. Then, barely young adults ourselves, we stood before a priest in front of hundreds of friends and family and exchanged our vows.

From that point forward we shared the same meal, bed, house, weekends, family.

Before we got married, Joe and I did something called Pre-Cana. It was a preparation course our church recommended. We sat in this couple's living room while their dark-haired toddler scooted around our feet.

We answered questions about how we'd spend the holidays, how we'd handle a budget, where we'd like to live.

No one asked what it would be like to have a special-needs child together.

A child who never sleeps, runs away every chance they have, screams swear words at the top of their lungs, struggles to make sense of the social landscape, takes medicine every day, gets suspended in middle school.

Would it have mattered? No. Probably not. But maybe it would have lodged something tiny and flickering in my subconscious. And when the day came and our son Jack was diagnosed with autism, I would have been more prepared.

The truth is, there are still moments where I feel tired of having my story tied up with his. After twenty-five years together we continue to navigate our own childhood baggage, different parenting styles, his traditions, my traditions.

Only a few days ago, we had a terrible argument.

We stood in the kitchen shouting at each other. I was angry and frustrated. At the exact same time, I wanted him to fold me in his arms and hold me.

What did we argue about, you ask? Everything. Nothing.

Teenagers, the holidays, money, autism.

What can I say? The clutter of life wears us down sometimes.

We didn't talk for the rest of the day. I hate this. So many things happened but I couldn't tell him because I was teaching him a good lesson about how right I was.

A squirrel got his head stuck in the birdfeeder, the UPS guy ran over a package on his way down the driveway, I heard an old song on the radio we both love.

It was as though none of it happened at all. Not the silly squirrel or the package or the song.

Nothing is real until I tell it to Joe.

Since we've met, we've argued about sunscreen, Oreos, the right way to boil pasta, the best kind of vacation, where we should spend Easter, how much a new couch should cost.

You will, too. I am sorry to say it, but it is true. You will argue.

For us, autism magnifies many of our disagreements. This is largely because when Joe and I argue, we are loud. There is yelling. Although we've worked very hard to change this cycle, we are far from perfect.

Jack's nervous system is closely tied to ours. If he suspects Joe and I are upset, he moves quickly into fight or flight. He starts to pace around us and rubs his hands together. He asks us over and over again if we're getting divorced. As you can imagine, this only adds to the distress.

Much like autism, there is no instruction manual for marriage. There is no how-to booklet for navigating the tricky waters of a combined life.

These are a few things we learned over time.

HAVE A PLAN

If you are a couple who argues the way we do, it helps to have a plan.

(If you are not a couple who argues the way we do, feel free to tell us how you do it.)

Our plan is pretty straightforward: If one of us feels like we're escalating, we drop the topic until we're calmer. This isn't easy by any means, but it helps keep us out from screaming matches.

(I've also heard of a technique where one person blurts out a funny word or a favorite vacation spot when tempers start to rise. We've never tried that.)

I am a person who wants to discuss things ad nauseam. (Joe's words, not mine.) I like to finish an argument. So, for me, the plan of interrupting a conversation in the middle because we're getting frustrated was, well, frustrating. I need to know we'll circle back at some point. We usually give it a few hours or a day at the most. By that time, whatever we were arguing about usually seems less important.

I VERSUS YOU

I read somewhere that the way we use language can be helpful in an argument. And no, I don't mean swearing at your partner in the heat of the moment! That is what you might consider *unhelpful*.

Specifically, I mean the use of two words: *I* and *you*.

I is vulnerable. *You* is righteous.

You makes the other person defensive.

I creates a space of ease, of discovery.

"You are always late!"

I really needed you.

"You never understand!"

I wish I could explain it better.

"You make me angry."

I am so frustrated right now.

I know, it seems like such an insignificant thing to change about the way you communicate, but try it.

Once I shifted my language even just this little bit during our arguments, I noticed my own nervous system was calmer.

DATE NIGHT

I know, I know. It's expensive. And hard to find someone to watch the kids. And a little inconvenient. Also, expensive.

Ever since our oldest son was two months old, Joe and I went out on Saturday night. In those days I worked, at first full-time and eventually part-time. And I looked forward to Saturday night all week.

I think, after taking care of infants and toddlers, I just wanted to be a wife. I wanted to have an uninterrupted conversation and eat without little fingers touching all my food. I wanted to wear a cute outfit and maybe some high heels. Once a week, for a few hours, I could do just that.

I know a lot of mothers—especially working mothers—feel guilty being away from their kids on the weekend. The way I see it, there are one hundred and sixty-eight hours in a week. Spending two or three with them connecting with your spouse is very worthwhile.

It doesn't have to be fancy. A meal at your local restaurant or a few hours over coffee in the bookstore.

As for someone to watch the kids, we usually worked with someone who was a little older—not your typical teenage babysitter from down the street. Someone from the kids' daycare or school.

Also, to keep myself from pushing it off, once we found a good sitter, I'd ask her to commit to every Saturday night. This way we had consistency and a routine that everyone, especially Jack, could count on.

GO TO BED ANGRY

Yes, you read that right. Go to bed angry.

In my experience, the whole do-not-go-to-bed angry is a crock-of-you-know-what.

The worst words we've ever said to each other were when the clock crept towards darkness. Remember when your mother said nothing good happens after midnight? She was right.

Go to bed. Lie there and think your dark, murderous thoughts. Listen to his breathing. Pull the covers tight and take your own deep breaths, in through the nose and out through your mouth.

You see, sleep is the elixir. It is the solution to many marital problems. You might not wake relaxed, but you will wake up ready to begin again. You will put waffles in the toaster. You'll get the kids on the bus. Life resumes.

Yes, you will argue. But you will come back to one another. Time and time again you will learn new ways to do this.

RUPTURE AND REPAIR

I don't know about you, but one of the worse feelings I have as a parent is when Joe and I have a big argument in front of the kids.

I immediately start to question myself. Who are we? What are we teaching them? Are we ruining their idea of marriage?

(Answers: We are human. We are teaching them that it's okay to argue. We are demonstrating that marriage is occasionally difficult.)

Still, even knowing this, I often have a pit in my stomach afterward.

I learned from a very wise person that exposing kids to what's called *rupture and repair* is actually good for them. It helps them understand that yes, grown-ups don't always use the right parts of their brain. We, too, get angry.

The emphasis here is on the *repair*. You want them to understand that a couple can disagree, and still come back to one another again.

This was especially important for Jack. If he sensed any kind of conflict between Joe and me, he started to worry we would get divorced. It shook him. We always made a point to tell him that yes, we argued, but we're fine now.

MARRIAGE COUNSELING

There were times in our marriage when Joe and I were stuck. I don't know how else to describe it. It felt as though we were recycling the same problems over and over again.

We've always had the same dynamic. As I mentioned, although not a couple who bicker regularly, we are prone to large (loud) outbursts. We have long stretches of oceanic calm, then a riptide of anger threatens to drag us beneath the waves.

After a particularly difficult argument, we found ourselves talking to a therapist—a kindly gentleman in his early sixties. He came highly recommended.

In a small office with tan carpeting, Joe and I sat side by side in armchairs and made our case for why we were right and other one was wrong.

In this room we untangled the baggage we brought into marriage. Family expectations and differences in parenting styles.

We discovered new ways to de-escalate our stormy moments and anticipate each other's moods. Together, we wept. We confessed to pressure we each feel in the face of five kids, of autism.

After every session, the kindly therapist said one thing as we walked out the door.

"Remember," he reminded us. "You love each other."

For me, I developed a new strategy where I remind myself *this is just a moment*. Recently Joe and I got a little, uh, *huffy* with each other in an airport. We were traveling with the kids and, after several delays, tensions were high. I relaxed back in my seat, folded my hands together, and reminded myself that this was simply a moment in time. It did not define our marriage, or Joe, or me.

THE LITTLE THINGS

In the beginning, I thought marriage should be full of fanfare. Elaborate anniversaries, flowers, romance. Not realistic, or sustainable. It isn't for us, anyway. Not the way of flowers. It is not the way of candy-coated Valentines, or Hallmark cards, or lavish birthday gifts.

It is the way of cleaning vomit from carpets. It is the way of burgers on the grill when I don't want to cook and waiting up for teenagers just licensed to drive.

It is the way of IEP meetings, and behavior plans, and guardianship appointments. It is the way of holding doors, and carrying bags, and always offering me the first bite of his chicken parmesan.

It is the way of the ordinary work it takes to move a family forward.

One time I was watching a movie. I said I was hungry. I got up to make a bagel, only to discover the toaster was broken. It would only work if you stood there and held the lever down.

Joe walked in and told me to go back to the couch. He held the lever down, toasted my bagel, and put lots of cream cheese on it—just the way I like it.

From that point forward I decided to focus on the small gestures he offers. The cup of coffee he makes me in the morning. The late-night snack while I'm writing. The way he fills my car with gas when I'm low.

Try it.

Once you start looking, they're everywhere. It will change the way you see each other. It will change the way you see your marriage.

BREATHE

Here is the thing—maintaining your marriage while raising small children is hard work. If you are in the thick of it right now, with fussy infants and busy toddlers and autism, it is normal to feel your marital ground shifting a little. Try not to panic. I can tell you, like most things in life, it gets a lot easier over time.

Breathe.

The day after our argument, Joe stood in my office. He untangled a set of lights I'd been meaning to hang, long strands with stars dangling from the bottom. Quietly, he undid the knots and loops until he had one string.

As afternoon faded outside the windows, he hung them.

I looked at my computer while he did this. I knew he was telling me something, but I wasn't ready to hear it.

There is no manual for marriage, it's true.

Marriage is small pockets of time—moments of hope, and love, and loss, all mixed up with old-fashioned grit.

Funny birthday cards, goofy texts, the silent treatment, stolen kisses, give-and-take, compromise, failed attempts, and new beginnings.

Morning coffee, smiles across the dinner table, pretty lights untangled.

It's just you, him, and this wildly ordinary life you are trying to build.

One day you will look up from your computer and see him standing before you, his hands full of stars.

You'll watch his silhouette against the dusky night and you will realize.

He holds up half your sky.

He holds up half my sky.

Nothing is real until I tell him.

Remember, you love each other.

CHAPTER 11

Finding a Program after High School

Jack walks around the room. He traces his fingertips along the windowsill, then the desk. He opens and closes drawers.

After overcoming a case of amblyopia—also known as lazy eye—by patching his right eye so the left may grow stronger, Jack's eyesight is strong. Yet it's almost as if he sees the world through his fingertips. He's always been this way.

It's fall of 2022. Outside the window, leaves drift lazily and collect on the ground like colorful confetti. We are in Philadelphia, dropping Jack's older brother off at college. Jack had just begun his senior year in high school.

Watching him circle the small space, I realize he

wants this for himself. He is visualizing college life, complete with a bed in a cramped dorm room. He is picturing himself here.

Up until that point, I hadn't though a lot about what Jack's future might look like. He had the option to attend high school until he was twenty-one, but that didn't feel like the right fit. He was working in a restaurant washing dishes and could probably increase his hours there, or perhaps take a class at a community college.

In retrospect, I'm surprised I hadn't given it more thought. When it comes to Jack, I am often in "planning" mode—trying to figure out the next step for him. For reasons I can't explain, I never looked much further than high school. Maybe it was because I never heard of a kid like him going to a college program, nor had I ever heard of one aimed at neurodiverse students.

Standing there with my arms full of new towels, I realized I had to try and see what was available.

Two days later, home again, I started to research. I sat down at my desk and typed **college programs for kids with autism** into my browser. A few links popped up, and I was on my way, down yet another

> *rabbit hole of obstacles, de facto discrimination, rejections, and, at the end of it all, a quiet hope.*
>
> *The first thing I learned is there are very few programs for kids like Jack—kids who aren't necessarily academically inclined, but still want to experience something close to college.*

When we start talking about the possibility of a program, Joe and I decided we wanted him within driving distance in case he needed us.

Also, based on some feedback from Jack after he finished a summer program between junior and senior year, we wanted to explore options that would allow him to be integrated into a neurotypical population from time to time, in addition to the supports he'd need.

At eighteen, Jack didn't drive a car. We could leave him alone for an hour or two at a time, but he hadn't yet learned how to occupy himself very productively. It would be nice if he could live in a small town or city where he could walk to stores, restaurants, or even a movie theater.

Although he was fairly far along in life skills such a cooking and laundry, he had a naivete about him that concerned me—especially when it came to managing money and understanding how to navigate crowds.

Ideally, a college program would have social and emotional supports, as well as coaching for increased life skills.

With these parameters in mind, I started with a website called www.thinkcollege.net. It's a resource for locating programs aimed at neurodiverse students and higher education. The tab labeled "Students and Families" brings you to a directory. At the bottom left-hand side is another button called "Advanced Filter." From here, I chose the location, type of diagnosis, and whether or not Jack wanted to take courses for credit.

It was a great starting point, but also humbling. The filter returned six programs that would match our requirements. Six, out of hundreds across the country.

On top of that, we were told spots were limited. Three, perhaps four, students were accepted a year.

I spent hours on the phone, leaving voice mails and asking for a call back. Once in touch with an actual person, I tried to ask questions to see if the program matched the website description.

Too often, they did not. One program director explained they lock up the food in between mealtimes. Another gentleman said that, despite what the website said, they expect students to complete a full course load with the intent of a degree at the end of four years.

For us, a degree wasn't necessarily the goal. We simply wanted

Jack to experience college life with some support—to share a room and eat in the dining hall and perhaps experiment with taking one or two classes.

At the same time, the clock was ticking. I felt the imminent pressure of the end of his senior year, when all services would come to a screeching halt.

What if he doesn't get in somewhere?

What if there is nowhere for him to go?

What will he do?

It's fair to say this process touched an emotional nerve more than once.

The programs had names like Strive, and Reach, and Sail, and Excel.

For some reason, the names themselves made me feel quietly unmoored.

On one hand, I was grateful they existed—grateful there are stops between full residential care and full-time college student.

On the other hand, would he be infantilized his whole life?

Round and round my mind circled.

The truth is, I thought this process would be fairly straightforward.

I thought we would identify a few programs and I'd help him apply and pass along the doctor's letter confirming that yes—yes!—this boy Jack does, indeed, have autism. My naivete, it seems, knows no bounds.

"Mrs. Cariello, after hearing more about your son, I'm afraid he doesn't fit the profile for our typical student."

"I'm sorry, Mrs. Cariello, we don't accept applicants if their parents have guardianship."

"We're full for the upcoming academic year. Perhaps you can try again next year."

These were just a handful of responses I heard. Each time, I fought the urge to throw the phone across the room. At times like this the seats at the proverbial table seemed few and far between for him.

Where was the seat for the tender teenager who comes home after school and carefully spreads salt on the driveway? Where were the pendants and the magnets in the mail, wooing him to one campus or another? Or the opportunities for the neurodiverse thinkers—the game-changers, the rule-breakers, the potential-seekers?

A local program caught my attention. Set to begin in March,

it was virtual, aimed at helping neurodiverse high school seniors begin the transition to college classes. Eagerly, I spoke with the director, and she agreed there was a spot for Jack. Yet after I sent the paperwork, she realized Jack would be seventeen at the start date. She called to explain applicants must be eighteen to enroll.

"He'll be eighteen in May, just two months later!"

Still, she insisted it wasn't possible.

I argued that many college students—myself included—started college at seventeen. It was simply the way his birthday fell on the calendar.

"I'm sorry, Mrs. Cariello. This is the way we've always done it."

This is the way we've always done it.

This was perhaps the most frustrating sentence I have ever heard.

This is where the work was.[1]

So often we were down during this process, but we were never

---

[1] I connected with a very knowledgeable educational consultant after I did the research for Jack's programs, but I greatly wish I'd found him sooner. Jordan Burstein and his mother founded JJB Consultants in 2010. It provides college placement services for students with learning differences like attention deficit hyperactivity disorder (ADHD), autism spectrum disorders (ASD), traumatic brain injuries, and developmental delays. You can find Jordan here: https://jjb-edconsultants.com.

out. As the leaves continued to fall, and the autumn landscape turned white with snow, I fervently hoped this ceiling would one day be the floor. And whenever I felt like giving up, I remembered his face, his fingertips, the drawers opening and closing.

After thoroughly investigating each of the six options, we narrowed it down to two. Coming from a small high school with a lot of guidance and support, I was certain Jack wouldn't be able commit to a full course load. And the goal was to increase his autonomy and independence, so I immediately crossed the program that locked food away off the list.

Four. The number felt flimsy. Insubstantial.

We began the application process. As I made appointments for psychological testing and filled out paperwork that asked about things like medication compliance and level of the autism diagnosis, I couldn't help but notice this was a stark contrast to the way my oldest son applied to college.

As for the process itself, I found staying organized was important. Though paperwork has never been my strong suit, I created a spreadsheet in Excel to keep track of who I spoke with, and when. I added notes and made sure to follow up with phone calls. Tedious, but worth it.

Instead of SAT (standard assessment test) scores, we had to submit psychological reports. Instead of essays, we filled out complicated forms about hygiene, safety, and guardianship agreements. It was a delicate balance of expressing his vulnerabilities while emphasizing his strengths.

Similar to the early days of IEP meetings, I found myself once again trying to spring my son to life from black and white words on paper.

He has severe anxiety, but he manages his own medication.

He makes the most delicious chocolate cake you've ever tasted, but he screams and circles the room if the fire alarm starts.

When he was eight he collected license plates. From Maine to Washington to Australia, people sent them until we had a wall full of them.

Carefully, Jack would sign his name to the bottom of the paperwork.

This was November of his senior year. Ideally, we should have begun at least a year sooner. As usual, time was not on our side. Faithfully, Jack checked the mailbox every day on his way home from school, waiting for an answer.

He was rejected from two right away. I was notified virtually, thankfully, so I could break the news to him gently.

"Dear Jack, we regret to inform you that you are not a good fit for our program at this time."

That was hard to tell him.

I mean, what is the right fit for someone who has followed an Individualized Education Plan every year of school, but has never once missed an opportunity to pick up extra hours at work?

What is the right fit for a boy who remembers every single birthday of every single person he's ever met?

Who longs to be a part of something bigger than his autism diagnosis?

"For Mom. What time will I be. A good fit."

After about a month, a third program suggested we wait a year. We were down to one and, set in rural farmland with a focus solely on life skills, it was our least favorite choice overall.

In the final hour, I got an email from Jack's school psychologist, recommending a place she'd heard about from another family. I typed the name into my web browser and started reading.

A residential space in the center of a small collegiate city, flanked by three schools. Forty-four neurodiverse students lived year-round in a large, pretty brick building. They shared suites with kitchens, as well as community areas and a dining room.

There were staff there from 7:00 am until 11:00 at night. Academic, social and emotional, and life skills coaching were all part of the scaffolding to help students begin to acclimate and build a more independent life.

Social outings were also a regular part of this program: bowling, camping trips, holiday parties, apple picking, bike rides around town. The overall goal was to begin building connections amongst the community.

Students choose from three nearby colleges.

It was almost too good to be true.

Holding my breath—literally and metaphorically—I called the office number and asked to speak with the director. After a few minutes, a man named Scott greeted me. We spoke for nearly an hour. He recommended we schedule a time to visit and begin the paperwork—with only a few spots left for the upcoming year, time was of the essence.

We arranged to visit the following week. Joe took the day off of work and we left early. The drive was a little over two and a half hours—falling well into our geographic range for distance.

> On the car ride, snowflakes dotted the frozen ground. Here and there, Christmas wreaths adorned

the doors to farmhouses and stores. Jack seemed excited. Quiet for the most part, every once in a while, he'd take out his ear buds to ask a question.

"I would live here?"

"Yes buddy. If you like it."

I was incredibly nervous. Once again, I felt the weight of the never-ending balancing act—hoping he was a good fit whilst also making sure they understood his vulnerabilities.

"Welcome, Jack," the young woman smiled as she opened the door. She gestured toward a couch inside her office. "Come, take a seat."

"This place," Jack said, "is VERY OLD."

"Jack!" I hissed.

He shot me a look. "I am sorry. I shouldn't have said that."

"No problem!" The program director said cheerily. "It is old! It was built in the 1800s. It's what called an old Victorian house."

For the first time in a while, I felt my shoulders relax. She seemed to, well, get him. A tiny flicker of hope shot through me. I looked over at Joe. He smiled back at me.

She asked a few questions about Jack's diagnosis, how he pictured his first year after high school, if he could take medication on his own. After a half an hour, she suggested a tour.

We followed her through the building—up winding staircases and long, narrow hallways, stopping in a dorm room so Jack could explore the space. Once again, I noticed him tracing the walls and the windowsills lightly with his fingers. Standing near the open door, he turned to us.

"Yes. Here. I could live here."

As we wrapped up the tour, I searched the director's face for clues. Did she like him? Was he a good fit? Would she recommend he be accepted? She gave nothing away. She simply smiled and wished us a safe drive.

Please, I silently implored. Please see beyond his remark about the building. See past the stimming. See that he is possible.

We came home, finished the rest of the paperwork, and waited for an answer. Jack continued to check the mailbox. The weeks that followed were a whirlwind of nervous excitement, tempered by a few humbling realities.

This program—and all the others I researched—is very expensive. Not including tuition, we pay $80,000 out of pocket. There is no financial aid. No scholarships or merit money.

As Joe and I wavered on whether or not this was the right fit, the cost weighed heavily on us. Though we could make it work with our budget, the pressure to make sure the program was a good fit was high.

Round and round we went at night, next to each other on the couch. What if he got accepted? Was he ready? Was this the best option? What if it didn't work out? Could we handle a mistake to the tune of $80,000?

In this case Joe and I measured success very differently. To me, a successful first year meant Jack could live away from us and take even the smallest steps toward independent living. Perhaps he could connect with a peer. I hoped he'd participate in the community activities and branch out of his comfort zone a little.

Joe's goals were more specific—practical. He wanted to see him take at least one college class. Manage his money independently.

So badly, I wanted someone to give us guidance. I wanted someone to look me in the eye and say firmly that sending Jack here was the right choice.

Three weeks later, a few days shy of Christmas, we got a letter.

Dear Jack, I am excited to offer you a spot in our program for the upcoming year.

Just like that, we were standing on our ceiling.

ADVOCACY

Gentle reader, we want this to improve. We need more programs, more options, more spots. This means we, as a community, must continue telling our own stories. We must do our own part to increase awareness that our kids deserve to build a life for themselves, whatever that may look like.

If compassion and inclusion is a house we build, then storytelling is the key to the front door.

> *Nearly two years after that afternoon in Philadelphia, our family stood together in another small dorm room. We unpacked kitchen utensils. We folded t-shirts and made the bed.*

And when we made our tearful goodbye in the parking lot, he turned one way and the rest of us turned the other.

Beneath a lemon-yellow sky in the beginning of July, my son Jack turned back to me. He asked a single question.

"Mom. Did you ever think this day would come?"

CHAPTER 12

The Road to Independence (or at Least to Moving Out)

> We did the research. We found the program. We signed the paperwork and organized our finances. Now what?
>
> The drop-off date was scheduled for mid-July. This seemed both close and far away at the exact same time.
>
> As winter's white landscape began budding green leaves, I started to consider how to stretch him even further in a few areas.

When you have a small child diagnosed with autism, it can be difficult to imagine they one day might not live with you anymore. I know when Jack was little, my proverbial crystal ball never quite forecasted beyond elementary school.

People often ask me what steps we took to begin the process of launching Jack from his childhood bedroom to a college program. Luckily, we had unintentionally paved the road in a few ways already.

SLEEPOVERS AND SUMMER CAMP

Jack has never been invited to a sleepover at a friend's house. Invitations to birthday parties were few and far between—in fact, I truly can't remember when he last received one.

Yet we knew he could sleep out of the house. From the time he was little, Jack would spend the night with Joe's parents every now and again. He would pack up his blue suitcase, climb in the car with Grandma and Grandpa, and not so much as glance back at me. They always stocked his favorite cookies and DVDs, and he had a ball.

When he was ten, we decided to send him to a weeklong summer camp with his brothers. We wanted him to experience a low-demand environment full of play. The counselors were young adults but big kids at heart, and the entire goal was to have fun. He resisted at first but wound up loving it and going three summers in a row.

THE ROAD TO INDEPENDENCE (OR AT LEAST TO MOVING OUT)

GOOD ROOMMATE/BAD ROOMMATE

We've always used the phrase *Bad Roommate Behavior* in our house to describe something inconsiderate—an empty milk container in the refrigerator, wet towels on the floor, an overflowing wastebasket in the bathroom.

As the July drop-off date grew closer, I started to have conversations around what a good roommate looks like in college as opposed to a bad roommate. In his new program we opted not to have him live in a single room, but to share a bedroom within a suite.

Jack had always shared a room at home. It was simply the way our house was set up—Rose had her own room and the boys all shared. Looking back, this was a good thing, as I felt better sending Jack into a shared situation knowing he had already experienced it.

What can be challenging is Jack's tendency to, uh, *police* people, if you will. He has a rather righteous side to him and likes to call out behavior he feels breaks the rules. His rules, anyway.

We had to balance between explaining what kind of good roommate he can be, while preparing him to tolerate different living styles within the program. Joe often encourages Jack to focus on what he can control—which is himself.

THE DINNER TABLE (AGAIN)

Ah, the dinner table. Community dining is a large part of the collegiate experience. Many kids with autism have trouble tolerating the sounds and smells of other people eating. As a result they eat in their rooms or after everyone else has finished.

As I mentioned earlier, our family made a point to sit together for dinner four to five times a week. We started when Jack was a toddler and, although it wasn't always easy, it paid off when thinking about sending him to a program.

MEDICATION

When he was about twelve, Jack started to manage his own medicine. As a rule follower, I knew he would administer it safely. At night I would hear him shake the small vial of pills into his hand and fill a cup with water. The same sounds marked the morning.

After a few years I told him it was his responsibility to remind me when he needed a refill. He did this by leaving the empty bottle on a small table in the hallway.

Most programs will ask if an applicant is what's called *medication compliant*, where they willingly handle their own medication and take it as the doctor prescribed. This is especially important for time-release prescriptions.

I recommend talking to your kiddo about exactly what he or she takes, the time of day that is recommended, and what the medication is aimed at accomplishing. In addition, review any side effects that may accompany a change in dosage.

Once Jack was accepted into the program we introduced him to the patient portal for the doctor's office. Through there, we had him order his own refills and manage the timing. For example, one particular medication needs to be ordered a few days in advance—or when he has a few pills left, so there isn't a gap.

Jack finds a weekly pillbox—the kind with a small box for each day of the week—helpful in keeping track of everything.

When he moved into his new space, one of the first things we did is locate a pharmacy within walking distance. Jack used the portal to change the address for his prescriptions.

IDENTIFICATION

This probably falls under the housekeeping category in terms of getting Jack ready, but it's something I didn't think of right away. Jack doesn't drive, which means he doesn't have a driver's license. Other than his passport, he didn't have any other form of government identification.

Shortly before he left, we made an appointment with the Department of Motor Vehicles for what's called a non-driver identification. It involved some paperwork and a few minutes getting his picture taken.

I think I underestimated how important this ritual was for him—he was very excited to receive his own laminated card the way his siblings with a license had. He immediately tucked it in his wallet.

UNTETHERING

Just as important as the practical steps for independence are the emotional strides we have to make. I call this process *untethering*. Medication compliance and money management weren't enough. I had to search for ways to make him emotionally independent as well.

In some ways our lives often revolve around our diagnosed children. This is no one's fault. It simply is. In addition to parenthood, we also manage the caregiving aspects of life—managing medication, therapies, and appointments.

When you have a diagnosed child, it can be easy to slip into a somewhat codependent relationship. We start to believe we are the only people who can safeguard our vulnerable child. We tell ourselves we are the only ones who can care for them—manage medication and help them get to sleep and prepare the food they enjoy.

And, of course, there is some truth to that.

THE ROAD TO INDEPENDENCE (OR AT LEAST TO MOVING OUT)

In considering this, I remembered a meeting that was held at Jack's elementary school years ago for special-needs parents. Amongst a few new changes like softer lights in the classrooms and a chance for our kids to walk through the hallways before the crowd of kids, the principal announced another policy: paraprofessionals, or classroom aides, would only work with students for one year. After that, the child would be assigned someone else for the following year. Groans erupted throughout the room.

I didn't think too much of it. Jack had been used to getting a new para each year and did fine with the change. But sitting at my desk so many years later, wondering how to best prepare him for something bigger than life inside our home, the conversation came back to me.

The truth is, in life alongside autism, progress isn't really progress if your kiddo can only perform for one teacher or person in their life. If he or she can only complete a worksheet, or sit through lunch, or pack their backpack if that person is present, it means they aren't mastering a skill that transfers across circumstances.

The same applies to motherhood. And while we certainly can't switch ourselves out for a new version year after year (can we?) it is important to consider all the ways your child will behave or complete a task just for you. This meant questioning habits and routines we'd created over the years.

Is he better at haircuts if you bring him? Does she eat what's for dinner if you cook it? Does he only brush his teeth if you're watching?

Although these are things more geared toward younger children, it's a good place to start stretching him or her to complete required tasks no matter who is present—a babysitter, aunt, or even grandma.

For instance, whenever I left the house without him, he was always standing in the doorway waiting for me as soon as I pulled into the garage. From the time he was little, he would watch for my car to pull up the driveway, stop whatever he was doing, and open the kitchen door. As soon as I stepped out, he asked me a million questions about where I'd been and who I'd seen.

Endearing? Absolutely.

Maddening? Perhaps a little.

I decided this would be a good place to start untethering us. That spring, I started pointing out how none of his siblings came to meet me at the door. They waited until I came in the house to greet me.

Like most things with life alongside autism, this was not successful at first. The first few times he was still waiting for me. Then I'd notice the door was open, but he was somewhere in the house. Each time, I'd reiterate that, as excited as I was to see him, I didn't want him waiting for me anymore.

THE ROAD TO INDEPENDENCE (OR AT LEAST TO MOVING OUT)

And that sentence was the heart of all this work. I didn't want him to wait for me forever. I wanted him to build his own life—one that included me less and less. As painful as that was for me to acknowledge as a mother, I knew it was important.

The first time I pulled inside and he wasn't standing there, I put my head on the steering wheel and cried. I couldn't help but question myself. What was I doing? Did this really matter?

It did. It does.

> *The work wasn't done once we dropped him off. From his very first day in the program, Jack texted us constantly. And I mean **constantly**. I'm talking twenty to thirty times a day. He'd ask what we were doing, tell us what he had for lunch, share about the latest celebrity news. It was excessive and, quite frankly, very disruptive.*
>
> *Jack's program allowed for six sessions with a parent coach[1]–someone who never met Jack, but just walked us through this big transition of launching him. Her name was Shannon.*
>
> *"I mean, he's texting us," I blurted out during our first phone call together. "Like, a **lot**."*

---

1 For more resources and strategies, check out Coach Shannon's website: www.shannonearlecoaching.com.

I was sitting in my car outside my favorite lunch spot—a little Vietnamese café known for hot pho and fresh rolls. The mid-summer sun danced across the dashboard.

"Okay," Shannon said gently. "That happens sometimes when kids first leave home."

She went on to explain that Jack's frontal lobe—the part of the brain responsible for thinking, emotions, personality, and decision-making—had been deeply intertwined with mine for a long time. I needed to begin the process of separating myself from him.

I confessed that Joe and I felt a little panicked—that maybe we sent him too soon and he couldn't handle it. It felt as though we'd sent a twelve-year-old into the world to live without us, which, in some ways, we did. I told her how worried I was that his anxiety and obsessive compulsive disorder might take over at any time and his team would recommend he leave the program altogether, and he would come home to live in our basement. Forever. To the tune of $80,000.

What can I say? I like to catastrophize. Going to the worst-case scenario feels comfortable to me, like wearing an old sweater on a cold day.

"Great," Shannon said. "You've told me all the things that could go wrong. Now tell me what could go right."

*I paused. What could go **right**? I never considered anything other than negative outcomes. That was my brain's default mode.*

"Well," I said slowly, "He could get acclimated there."

"Yes!" she agreed. "He absolutely could settle down soon."

"He could respond to some limits around communication."

"Yep, he could. Keep going!"

"He might actually build a life there."

"Carrie, yes. He might actually build a life there."

He might actually build a life there.

The words circled my mind for the rest of the afternoon.

MOVE FROM A WE TO AN I

Once at home, I sat down at my desk with my bowl of steaming noodle pho. I leaned back in my chair and thought about what Coach Shannon said. It was time to move from a *we* to an *I*. I connected the tips of my thumbs together to form a *W*. Slowly, I moved them apart, tucking everything but my pointer fingers against my palm. Two *Is*. It seemed simple enough, in hand gestures anyway.

In everyday life, *We-to-I* requires some practical steps. First off, we told Jack we would only be available by text during a certain window, like from noon until 1:00. This took a few weeks for him to really stick to, but the messages did start dwindling from a dozen every couple of hours to one or two an afternoon.

For my own sanity, I started to utilize Coach Shannon's strategy and focus more on what I call *Whole Brain Thinking*. Whenever I'm tempted to catastrophize. I allow myself to take a moment and make the full list of what could go wrong. Then I make a list of everything that is possible.

DUALITY (AGAIN)

I talk a lot about the difference between physical age and emotional age—something I call the autism duality. For so long, it was easier to address Jack's emotional age.

THE ROAD TO INDEPENDENCE (OR AT LEAST TO MOVING OUT)

I always called him *big guy*.

"Come on big guy, it's time for school."

"Hey big guy, we need to stop at the grocery store."

Once the idea of a college program came on the horizon, I started to adjust the way I addressed him. I was worried that if I infantilized him, the rest of the world would too.

Jack also reached for our hands in the parking lot—even as his height climbed and he started to tower over Joe and I. I never minded the stares. I knew it was for comfort more than safety.

But what would he do when he was walking in a parking lot without us? Or on his way to the bookstore, or to get ice cream with peers from his program? I needed him to know he could walk alone.

Untethering. It is a word wrapped around a stop sign.

I stopped ordering for him in a restaurant—or following up his order with a look to the server to make sure he or she understood him.

I stopped suggesting what clothes he should wear.

I stopped monitoring how much soda he drank or how many cupcakes he ate when we were at a holiday party or a barbecue.

I stopped calling him *Big Guy.*

Gentle reader, this was hard for me. For so long I was his soft landing, his safe place, his voice.

But he is not my friend. He is not my companion. He is my son.

He could actually build a life there.

> About three months into his program, Jack came home for a visit. In the days prior, I texted him off and on—reminding him to pack things like his medication, his bathing suit. After a few exchanges, he texted me back a collection of words so simple, they made me catch my breath.
>
> "Mom, I've got this."
>
> In life alongside autism, our triumphs may look different. Yet they are there all the same.

Discussion Questions

Chapter 1—Papercut Days: Autism and Grief

- What are some ways you take care of yourself when you feel grief come on?
- Who did you first tell about the autism diagnosis and why?
- Do you catastrophize?

Chapter 2— Autism and Food: How to Have Success at the Dinner Table

- How did your partner grow up eating dinner? How did you?
- Do you agree on what your own family's mealtimes should look like?
- Does your family have any games they like to play at the table?

Chapter 3—How to Prepare for Family Gatherings

- In this chapter I talk about preparing the host for your arrival. What would you add to this list?
- Do you have a toolbox answer for uncomfortable questions?
- Can you find your own ways to relax at a family party?

Chapter 4—Autism Siblings

- Is there a way your neurotypical children help with your diagnosed kiddo's progress?
- Has your family experienced "leapfrogging?" How do you handle it?
- What special ways do you have to make time for each child?

Chapter 5—Strategies for Money and Budgeting

- Is your kiddo struggling to understand money?
- Do you and your partner agree on a budgeting strategy?
- What would you add to the Budgeting Umbrella?

Chapter 6—Puberty

- How is puberty going so far?

DISCUSSION QUESTIONS

- What are you finding helpful when it comes to managing hormones and behavior?

- What do you think of the explanation of a tantrum versus a meltdown?

Chapter 7—How to Give the Sex Talk

- When you were a kid, who gave you the "Sex Talk?" Was it helpful?

- What are some things your hope your child will come away with after your discussion?

Chapter 8—Autism, Dating, and Social Media

- When it comes to your neurodiverse kiddo and dating, what worries you the most?

- We had Jack come up with a "toolbox"—or list of things to do before he meets someone in person that he connected with online. What would you add to this list?

Chapter 9—Raising a Whole Child

- Are you or your partner acting like "The Person?" How does that make you feel?

- What "soft skill" are you hoping to teach your child outside of the IEP table?

- What do you think of the idea of loving our kids through their difficult moments?

Chapter 10—Tips for Marriage

- When it comes to your marriage, is there one particular area where you feel "stuck" right now?

- When do you feel most connected to your partner?

- How are you able to carve out space for your marriage on a daily basis?

Chapter 11—Finding a Program after High School

- What kind of program are you interesting in finding for your kiddo?

- Is he or she a part of the process?

- What do you hope for most?

Chapter 12—The Road to Independence (or at Least to Moving Out)

- When it comes to your diagnosed child, what does independence mean to you?

- What does it mean to your child?

- Instead of catastrophizing about all that might go wrong, can you consider what may go right?